The Aunts

The
Aunts

By Isabella Halsted

The Sharksmouth Press
1992

Cover photo: *The Five Curtis sisters, c. 1895: Frances, Elinor, Isabella, Harriot, Margaret*
Frontispiece: Isabella, Frances, Margaret, Elinor, Harriot
Back cover: Picking grapes in the orchard at Manchester
Photograph of the author by Nancy Scanlan

© Copyright 1992 by
The Sharksmouth Press
Manchester, Massachusetts
Second Edition, 1993.
Printed in the United States of America
ISBN 0-9636116-0-7

Contents

Preface

My mother Isabella (Hopkinson) Halsted was the third daughter—the middle child—of five girls born to Charles and Elinor Hopkinson of Manchester, Massachusetts. She was born and grew up in a forty-acre paradise of woodlands, craggy shoreline and sparkling sea overlooking Massachusetts Bay, twenty miles northeast of Boston as the gull flies.

The land had been purchased by her grandfather Greely Curtis, soon after his marriage to Harriot Appleton in 1863. There he built a great stone summer house for himself, his wife and their ten children, as well as a smaller cottage nearby to house his spinster sisters in the summertime, as well as other guests. The ten children—five boys and five girls—had a comfortable and mostly untroubled upbringing, in Boston in the winter, at the Manchester house in the summertime.

In due course the five sons went their separate ways, but the five Curtis daughters stayed close to home. In 1903 Elinor, the only daughter of Greely and Harriot to wed, married Charles Hopkinson, and they built a fine new house a few hundred yards away from her parents' house.

The Hopkinsons' house stood—and stands—on a bluff eighty feet above the sea, just above a dramatic jutting granite promontory whose thrusting sharp-edged profile gives it the appearance of a voracious sea-creature lunging at its prey. "Sharksmouth" was the name given to the rock formation, and subsequently to the entire forty-acre estate. Other houses were added to the property over the years, but the sense of the place remains very much as it was 130 years ago.

Almost my first childhood memories are of Sharksmouth, or "Manch," where my family regularly spent its summers—learning to swim, to ride a bicycle, to turn hand-cranked ice cream, to swing a tennis racquet, to pull weeds endlessly in the vegetable garden. I fell in love and courted my wife at Manch. Summer after summer we came back, no matter where we lived the rest of the year.

So we have this place in our bones, for better or for worse. Our children are the fifth-generation descendants of Greely and Harriot Curtis, who gave the place its start.

But it was Greely and Harriot's four unmarried daughters— the "Aunts" of the title—, together with our grandparents Elinor and Charles Hopkinson, who really gave it its enduring soul. Every year from early spring to late autumn, they occupied it and put their stamp on it over a span of more than a century. (They spent their winters in Boston at "Twenty-eight"—28 Mt. Vernon Street, a house on Beacon Hill their parents had acquired soon after their marriage).

Along with my brother and sisters and the innumerable cousins who were our contemporaries each summer at Manch, I never knew the aunts as young women; they were all old when we were first aware of them (the youngest, Aunt Pedge, was born fifty years to the day before me). We knew them as formidable, eccentric, sometimes even forbidding, but they did not play a central role in our lives.

It was a different matter for our mothers.

Isabella Hopkinson and her four sisters were in almost daily contact with the Aunts, who taught them, as they taught later generations, how to play tennis and golf, how to handle a canoe, and how to swim. They also provided them with a rich offering of the great range of possibilities life could offer.

I doubt if they taught their nieces how to dance, to flirt, to seek out boys, or what it means to fall in love. Spinsters all, the Aunts' lives may have been in that respect incomplete, but the wide-ranging careers each of them pursued in her own way amply made up for the fact that none of them ever married. They were pioneers, unafraid to tackle new territory, in fields of endeavor from politics to education to golf and tennis.

But *how* they lived those pioneer lives was just as important as their many accomplishments. Even as a child, I knew that these women placed great store in integrity. It was nothing they preached; they just showed it by everyday example. A forthright, no-nonsense approach to life was what mattered. Flattery and frills did not.

Such was the legacy they passed on to their niece Isabella, along with an enduring admiration and respect for these four extraordinary people that is reflected in every page of her loving memoir. She recounts how the Aunts helped raise her and her sisters as children, but she also had many opportunities to visit them and plumb their memories in their later years. Divorced from our father in 1952, she lived alone in Cambridge from then on, just across the river from Boston and "Twenty-eight." Between 1961 and 1967 she was the director of the Boston Center for International Visitors, with its headquarters at 55 Mt. Vernon, almost across the street from the Aunts. She often stayed at the Stone House at Manchester with the surviving Aunts, or dropped in on them at odd moments to chat.

It is no surprise, therefore, that she developed both a strong interest in telling their stories and a unique perspective on their full and fascinating lives and the influences that shaped their characters. Over the last nine years she has been recording these recollections, together with historical data and family anecdotes painstakingly gleaned from thousands of letters, diaries, photographs, newspaper clippings and other memorabilia. The Aunts never threw anything away.

The photographs included in this volume are only a handful of the thousands of snapshots and more formal portraits left behind by the Aunts, offering random glimpses into the lives and times of the Curtis children as they grew up. Most of the pictures were taken by their mother, a prolific enthusiast in the early days of photography. Each year, on the fourth of July, Mrs. Curtis would set up her cumbersome tripod and hefty view camera to photograph the ten children, their faces, their clothing, their pets, their surroundings reflecting the aura of a bygone time. She lined them up by age: solemn Billy on the left, then Fanny, Elly, Greely, on down to little Peggy, a white blur not quite caught by the slow shutter speed and emulsion on the glass negative plate in Mrs. Curtis' camera. Other photos have captured glimpses of how they lived: the horses, the first automobile, an afternoon sail on Greely's yacht *Dream*, Aunt Bog's Island, and their many trips to Europe. They were pasted into dozens of scrapbooks unearthed from closets and bureau drawers, along with many more albums of photographs collected and taken by Isabella Curtis. They provide a rich complement to the written narrative.

Some readers may have other memories and perspectives on the character and accomplishment of the Misses Curtis. But as one who knew and followed them from the prime of their lives until one by one they passed away, Isabella Halsted is superbly qualified to tell their story.

Thomas A. Halsted
Manchester, Massachusetts, January 15, 1993

The family at breakfast
Manchester, c. 1887

Chapter One

Family

When the last of the ten children of Greely and Harriot Curtis was approaching the age of ninety, I often kept her company during the winter of 1971, staying weeks at a time in the old family house on Beacon Hill. Aunt Hat had been National Women's Golf Champion in 1906, and still climbed two flights of stairs several times a day, went to the Symphony on Friday afternoons, wrote postcards, terse and to the point, to her relatives and friends, and enjoyed playing cards. One Sunday, she looked up from an article in the *New York Times* on early aviation developments, and said, "Pa never wanted Steen to go into aeronautics." She read a bit more. Then, discarding the article, she announced with finality, "We have no use for the Wright Brothers." In the silence that ensued, I thought of her father (my grandfather). Was he a particularly domineering martinet, or was he a typical Victorian paterfamilias? Her remark about the Wright Brothers fascinated me, not only because of the shadow cast on the famous pioneers; I was also charmed by the vitality of Curtis family solidarity her words conveyed, and her vigorous use of the present tense.

Aunt Hat was the ninth of the ten children. There were five sons and five daughters. No wonder she spoke of the family in the present tense, for she had never married and had lived at home all her life with three other sisters. Home, in the winters, was in Boston, at 28 Mt. Vernon Street, but the rest of the year it was at Manchester, in a Victorian-Gothic castle beside the sea, surrounded by generous acreage of woods and farmland.

My mother was the only Curtis sister to marry, and as she and my father had built their house close by on the family land, "the Aunts" played a large part in my growing years and for years thereafter. We took the Aunts for granted when we were children. They were built-in companions and care-takers for my sisters and me. They taught us to swim and play tennis, they took us berry-picking and skating. They brushed our hair fiercely, made jokes, did picture puzzles with us. They were always *there*.

After we grew up, went off to college, married and were busy with our own families, the Aunts were no longer a daily part of living, but I continued to see them frequently. As the decades roll by, I no longer take them for granted; emergence of women today casts a new light on the activities of these four maiden ladies.

The Aunts were the misses Frances, Isabella, Harriot and Margaret Curtis: Aunt Fan, Aunt Bog, Aunt Hat and Aunt Pedge. Their lives spanned more than a century, from 1867 to 1974. Their father, Colonel Greely Stevenson Curtis, had been a cavalryman in the Civil War who had retired early, due to malaria. In 1863, he married Harriot Appleton, daughter of Nathan Appleton, financier, congressman, very successful industrial pioneer. After their marriage and prolonged honeymoon in Europe, the couple bought the property on Beacon Hill and the acres bordering the sea at Manchester.

The Aunts, therefore, grew up in very comfortable circumstances, in the full flowering of the Victorian age. Their mother was of the crème-de-la-crème of Boston society, decorously raised at 39 Beacon Street. Their father, after his marriage, was a gentleman of leisure, possessed of fine horses, a yacht, a commodious city house and a large country estate. There was every reason to expect the Curtis daughters to be elegant young ladies, modestly sitting at home pursuing their embroidery, music and French lessons while awaiting gentleman callers of appropriate breeding.

Then why was Aunt Fan at age sixty on top of a step-ladder washing windows half-an-hour before lunching with Lady Astor? Why was Aunt Bog creosoting caterpillar nests? Why was Aunt Hat a dean at Hampton Institute for Negroes, and Aunt Pedge driving a Model T through bomb-smoldering French villages in World War I? Was it heredity or environment, or both, that accounted for their behavior? Probably both. Certainly environment accounted for much of it. Growing up in a family of ten lively and competitive children, the need for individual expression would be urgent. Each aunt had her own distinctive idiosyncrasies and displayed them vigorously in words and actions. The influence of heredity was not so blatant, but heredity certainly permeated the Aunts' home surroundings.

That winter of Aunt Hat's ninetieth year when I kept her company, I had ample time to muse on the influence of heredity and environment, for while she was napping, I explored at leisure that bounteous Boston house—bounteous in proportions, bounteous in contents. Two houses had been made into one, back in 1865. The sun poured in the southern bay windows overlooking the large back yard. Five stories of rooms were copiously furnished, and every bureau, desk and closet was filled with decades of daily living, for the Curtis family seldom threw anything away.

Soon I was as prone as Aunt Hat to make the past the present, for when I began opening cabinets and closets and bureaus, more decades were revealed, their modern and ancient symbols jumbled together as if all time were simultaneous. A Civil War sword clattered to the closet floor when I pushed aside some well-worn dresses of 1920 to 1950 vintage; in a bureau drawer, under strata of golf tees and score cards, a pretty girl with one coquettish curl on her shoulder smiled up from a little miniature with 1775 engraved on its golden back.

Time whirled into a bewildering and shining maelstrom in the niches and drawers of desks. Here were letters in wanton drifts and others in neat little packets lovingly tied with faded ribbons. The first I drew from its delicately small envelope was datelined Paris, 1802, in exquisite script: "Yesterday, we hired a chaise and drove out to the Faubourg XX..., still a shambles since Robespierre's rabble." Eye-witness accounts bring history alive, as all news media know. As I plunged through jumbled documents and letters, I lived through three centuries. I was there with that first Curtis immigrant when he killed a great she-bear threatening the village of Boston, and when his son was killed by Indians. I was there, throwing tea into Boston harbor and firing on Redcoats at Concord Bridge. I was mending my gunnysack on a barque carrying ice to Brazil; I was dancing with the Prince of Wales; I was feeling crowded below decks on the "Constitution" in 1814, and delighted with a new bonnet in 1825. I was there in St. Augustine when the Spanish flag was lowered and the Stars and Stripes went up. I dug for gold in Feather River and held the Indians at bay in the Northwest Territory, and I gathered oysters for supper as I strolled the beach at Newport.

Clearly, there was plenty of heredity in the closets and desks the Aunts used every day, even though they took it all for granted. They had little time for the past, being fully and briskly occupied with the present.

Let's drop in on them some winter morning in the 1930's, say, and see who's at home. The front door of 28 Mt. Vernon St. still has its brass plate engraved "G.S.Curtis" and is unlocked all day. (The key to the inner door of the vestibule is always kept behind the mailbox, ready for family and intimates.) As we enter we hear from the parlor, upstairs, a voice inquiring gently, "Ah-ha?" Aunt Fan has heard the key and wants to know who's there. We mount the stairs to the upper hall, where a wide doorway on the left opens into the sunny dining-room. A string of sleighbells hangs by the doorway, waiting to announce dinner. There is a big, round mahogany table and many chairs. Over the fireplace hangs a portrait of Nell Gwynn in blue velvet, sniffing a flower. It may have been painted by Sir Peter Lely. Beneath her, on the black marble mantel, is a bronze clock with .claw feet, topped by a brooding statue of Lorenzo di Medici, and matched on either side by bronze lamps, originally fueled by whale oil, but now adapted to electricity. In the glass-fronted cabinets flanking the fireplace are cut-glass goblets (never used by the abstemious Aunts), Rose Medallion Chinese teacups, and an apricot and gold coffee set, brought from Paris in 1815 or so. The south side of the room, facing the yard, is a graceful curve set with potted plants. Above the pier table hangs a portrait of James Freeman Curtis, the Aunts' grandfather, painted some

4

twenty years after he was a midshipman aboard the "Constitution." He is in high collar and stock of the 1830s, handsome, thin-faced, with forward-brushed side-whiskers, and direct gaze. What he looks down on now are those potted plants—not blooming, but here and there deceptively flashing pink because an Aunt has snatched from a neighbor's trashcan some wire-stemmed plastic flowers, botanically indefinable. Actually, they were snatched several years ago, but are now permanent; their rusty stems get watered every morning while Aunt Hat waits for breakfast to be sent up on the dumb-waiter. (Its on-coming rumble almost drowns out the cook's wild cry, "Oh-h Keh!" from the kitchen below.) On the last wall hang the portraits of Dr. and Mrs. Nathaniel Coffin, painted by Gilbert Stuart. They were great-great-grandparents of the Aunts. Between them hangs a darkening canvas of a lady in post-Elizabethan dress, holding on her lap a little girl. Although some authorities believe she was painted in America, in the 1680s, it has come down through the family from generation to generation that Mrs. Padeshall was painted much earlier, in London, after her husband had set sail for the New Land, and before he was killed by the Penobscot Indians. Near the corner hangs a portrait of Nathan Appleton, the Aunts' other grandfather and father-in-law of the poet Longfellow. On the floor by the windows is a Canton China vegetable dish full of drinking water for the dogs.

In the parlor, the furniture is mostly upholstered in blue velvet, and there is a grand piano. There is a telephone, with long stem and trumpet of early vintage, and a very long cord, long enough to reach across the room to any chair or sofa. Aunt Fan is seated, rather upright, in a blue armchair. Her feet are planted firmly parallel and about a foot apart. She is reading a detective story, at this unlikely morning hour. This does not mean that she has not already opened her mail, read the paper, chatted with the cook and ordered the day's meals; she has also whizzed around to the World Peace Foundation, down the street, to have a word with her devoted protegée who is secretary there.

Aunt Bog comes in, shuffling slightly, as she is apt to have a lame knee. She has been feeding her goldfish, one of whom is named Nina M. Tiffany, after a teacher they all had had, some fifty years earlier, when they studied in the School Room, at home, instead of going to schools. Aunt Bog pauses to exclaim, "Well, 'pon my word! And wot may *you* be doing in town so early in the morning, if I may make so bold?"

Aunt Hat is at the desk in the School Room, dashing off a postcard or two before she goes out. She will take the subway, change cars underground for the one that goes under Boston Harbor to East Boston, where the Maverick Dispensary, of which she is a founder, provides outpatient healthcare to many of the Italian families that make this section of the city a little Italy. "I'm off to Easta-Bost," she says, rising, "and France, do tell Margaret we don't want HOT applesauce with our pork for lunch." "Ah-ha," replies France, her eyes still on her detective. Aunt Hat starts for the door, but it is blocked massively by Aunt Pedge, clothed in a flowery crepe dress, bare legs ending in woolen socks and men's saddle shoes. She is large in the bust, but tapers to trim hips, shapely athletic legs. She has been three time National Women's Golf Champion.

"Pedgy! WHAT are you doing in that get-up! You're a sight!" is Aunt Hat's parting remark, squeezing past her. "Am I?" replies Pedgy mildly. "Well, I'm only going round to Mabel's, and then a twelve-o'clock meeting at Family Welfare—and France, be sure lunch is ready at one, so we can be through promptly; bridge starts at two, at Evelyn's." "Ah-ha," replies Aunt Fan; she closes her book and gets to her feet, addressing me. "Scrib, now you're here, have you got half a mo to pin up my dress properly?" She stands, displaying a bulky green and blue woolen garment, almost reaching the floor, and overgenerous across the shoulders. The belt is missing. "I found it yesterday, in the Basement, among the Stylish Stouts." She means Filene's Basement, the famous emporium of Boston, where goods that haven't sold upstairs are relegated to bargain status. "Here are the pins, my girl. My right shoulder has always been lower than my left; see what you can do." She stands upright, facing the window, shoulders squared and arms hanging at her sides, with perfect confidence that I can make her a model of fashion. Something about her posture and stillness, eyes gazing straight ahead, suggests the hours and hours she spent trying on dresses back in the late 1880s, when she was a beautiful and sought-after young lady, with bustle, fan and piled-up hairdo. It is touching. I begin to adjust the right shoulder, pinching together all the extra bulk of blue-green plaid, trying to avoid getting pins through whatever she has on underneath. I pin up the hem, and then I am ready to sew the new boundaries on the sewing-machine. To my amazement, Aunt Fan briskly unbuttons her new dress, and it slides to the floor—right in the parlor! Where a friend might drop in unannounced at any time! Aunt Fan is not revealed immodestly, however; she is fully clothed in a neat maid's uniform of plum-colored alpaca. "This is just a cast-off of Sarah's," she says. "Very cosy. I always wear it in cold weather." This aunt is the lady who spends evenings at the opera, who dines with the president of Harvard University, who served thirteen years on the Boston School Committee.

The Aunts had numerous friends. Some were fellow-champions of the civic causes they espoused, and others co-board members of charitable institutions they worked for. There were also "lame ducks." These included lonely spinsters and librarians, a discouraged policewoman, and a sprightly southern lady with a cleft palate whose humorous remarks only the Aunts could fully comprehend. But strongly imbedded in the Curtis family philosophy was the belief that life is to be enjoyed, and many people dropped in for the pure pleasure of swapping anecdotes and laughter in that pleasant welcoming parlor at 28 Mt. Vernon Street. Among the casual callers were Joseph Lee, instigator of playgrounds for Boston's schools; Mark Howe, essayist and historian; Judge Fred Cabot, founder of the Juvenile Court System; and Helen Storrow, for whose husband Storrow Drive is named.

"Twenty-Eight" (as the Aunts always called their Boston house) was also the setting for many social gatherings. Though they occasionally held decorous dinner-parties in the evening for distinguished guests, the Aunts did a lot of their entertaining at lunch time. Often one or another of them held a meeting of her sewing circle or lunch club, and on other days there was apt to be a friend or relative sharing the noonday meal. Cousin Sum was often present. He was William Sumner Appleton, a first cousin of the Aunts. Devoted to his "Aunt Harriot," their mother, during her lifetime, he had become an habitué of the household, dropping in several times a week for a meal and to sit humming to himself while he clipped interesting items out of the Aunts' newspaper. He was the founder of the Society for the Preservation of New England Antiquities, and for many years its chief administrator. He lived just down the street from the Aunts in bachelor quarters filled with New England relics and newspaper clippings. Cousin Sum had never married, but it seemed he maintained fantasies about the opposite sex. Of course these never surfaced at the Aunts' lunch table, where the conversation breezed along as heartily as did the eating of good food. However, his longings were expressed in bizarre fashion on Christmas day.

Every year, family members came from near and far to celebrate Christmas at "Twenty-Eight." They arrived late in the afternoon, in time to exchange presents before the traditional evening feast. In our grandmother's time, splendid presents were carefully chosen, appropriate to each recipient. After we were grown, the exchanges were a bit more slap-dash. Aunt Fan was apt to hand out gloves and woolen socks to everybody. She had got them in Filene's bargain basement, but never mind; it was the thought that mattered. Besides, all the Aunts, as grand-daughters of very rich Nathan Appleton, had been brought up to know that money should be used to help the unfortunate of this world—not to be squandered on people who could get along on their own. Aunt Hat splurged on peanut brittle, handing it out to one and all. Aunt Pedge usually dug around in her top bureau drawer to find presents: a leather notebook with pencil attached, a coin purse or two, and maybe a Czechoslovakian satchel, brightly embroidered. Aunt Bog did little joining in. She could be generous and sympathetic with individuals at quiet times, but she didn't like crowds. Of course we all reciprocated with modest gifts to them of home-made fudge and sachets stuffed with verbena or bay leaves.

Then came Christmas dinner. The dining room table, with damask cloth and silver candelabra, was stretched to full length and extra tables were set in the hall to accommodate all nieces, nephews and cousins. Everybody was dressed to the nines, in their best evening clothes. The dinner was always the same every year, and was magnificent: oyster soup to start with, roast goose with all the fixings, and for dessert, ice cream and plum pudding.

After dinner, we all trooped into the parlor again, and Aunt Pedge organized a simple competitive game. The many young females, both married and single, were encouraged to toss a tennis ball into a waste-basket set against the further wall. By the time the champion ball-tosser had been determined, the dining room was ready for the next event. The maids had cleared away all traces of dinner and everything was back to normal except the dining table. Its broad mahogany expanse was now almost completely covered by feminine underwear. Here were filmy nightgowns, flowery negligées, slips and petti-coats and panties trimmed with lace. All were luxurious enough to satisfy a latter-day Mme. de Pompadour or perhaps outfit a high-class house of ill-repute. This extraordinary display had been tenderly laid out by Cousin Sum, while the ball-tossing competition had been going on in the other room, and he now stood leaning by the side-board as all his younger female cousins trooped in. Led by the champion ball-tosser, who of course had first choice, they all circled the table, each picking out an exotic gift, while Cousin Sum smiled and smiled. No happening could have been more inappropriate in the Aunts' house than this one. Yet year after year they allowed it to happen. "Sumner's intimate undies," as they breezily called this annual rite, was an integral part of the Aunts' Christmas celebration. After all, Sumner Appleton was their cousin.

The Aunts also held charade parties at "Twenty-Eight" to which a lot of old friends came prepared to make fools of themselves if necessary. One charade I remember laughing at was of a three-syllable word: when the velvet curtains between the parlor and the school-room parted, they revealed Elise Vaughan, in semi-Egyptian head-dress, enthroned, and holding a writhing bit of string to her bosom before she toppled over onto the floor. That was Scene I, the first syllable. Scene II demonstrated the other two syllables acted together: six or eight of these proper Bostonians reeled, sang ballads, and shouted at each other in the best Irish brogue they could mimic. Have you guessed the word, good reader? You certainly will, when I describe the Finale, the enactment of the whole word: the curtains again part to reveal Aunt Hat flat on a hospital bed (actually three chairs), with a sheet over her evening dress, and a nurse attending. In comes Joe Lee. Though Chairman of the Boston School Committee, he is now disguised as a surgeon, in white coat and cap. He is accompanied by historian Mark Howe, similarly clad, as his medical consultant. "Let's see how that incision is getting along," says Dr. Joe to the nurse. She draws back the sheet, and the doctors gaze at Aunt Hat's stomach. One forgets its discreet covering of evening-dress as Joe Lee, moving one hand closely over it, ingeniously makes through hissing teeth, the savage sound of adhesive tape being pulled off bare flesh. "Excellent! Excellent!" he exclaims. "It's healing perfectly." "It's going to leave a very neat scar," Dr. Howe says, congratulating him, and they turn to go. "But what about her sedation for tonight?" asks the nurse. "Oh, I don't think she'll need any more sedation, but if she wakes up and is restless, you might give her a couple of _____," he instructs the nurse. End of scene. (The word, as I am sure you have guessed, is *aspirin*.)

Joe Lee, like the Curtises, loved river-skating as much as charades. If it was a sparkling winter day, and the ice thick enough, he and Charlie Jackson and Aunts Fan and Hat would drop everything else, take the train out to Dedham or further and spend glorious hours swooping upstream in long rhythmic arcs on the beautiful black ice of the Charles River. The Aunts had skates that clamped onto their regular, high-laced walking-boots. When they got to the river, they sat down on the bank and secured the skates to their boots with a skate key. The same skates served them for decades, but Aunt Fan at last tired of them; on her 75th birthday she gave herself a present—a pair of modern boot-skates, because, she explained, she was afraid no one else would think to do so.

Enthusiasm for outdoor sports came naturally to the Aunts, beginning in childhood, when they and their lively brothers were together much of the time, both indoors and out. It is plain that the Curtis parents felt that group activity was far healthier for growing children than individual occupations wherein solitude might lead to introspection. Moreover, their father, ever nostalgic for the Civil War years when he was an army officer, frequently barked out commands to his platoon of children.

During the winter months, the backyard of 28 Mt. Vernon Street became a community playground for many children of the Beacon Hill neighborhood. In freezing weather, the yard was flooded, making an ample hockey rink. When the ice melted, the neighbors came to play Prisoner's Base and One Old Cat. The yard was fine for winter games, but the real sporting activities began after the family moved down to Manchester in the spring. Here the playground was eighty-five acres, and the Curtis family activities expanded freely. There were woods and open fields, gardens and orchards, bordered on the south side by a quarter-mile of seashore. There were horses to ride, a yacht, swimming and boating, and a baseball field. Later on, a tennis court was built, and after the Essex County Club was established, all the Curtises took up golf enthusiastically. The club was only a mile away, and all the boys and girls had bicycles.

The place at Manchester was really home for the Curtises, since they lived there from April until the end of November, and often stayed on well into December. Though the boys married and lived elsewhere later, they returned to visit year after year; and of course their sisters were there perennially. The estate was named "Sharksmouth" for an upreach of jagged rock on the ocean's edge—a gigantic slab, slanting skyward, forming beneath it a mawlike cave of orange granite. Slightly inland and to the west of this landmark stood the Curtis house, on the brow of a wooded ridge overlooking the sea.

In 1865, soon after the Curtis parents had returned from their extended honeymoon in Europe, they visited the Danas in Manchester. Richard Henry Dana, father of the author of *Two Years Before the Mast*, was the first "summer resident" of Manchester, and owned shoreland, a beach and island east of the town. Greely Curtis, riding through the woods one day, reined in his horse on a pine-covered cliff set back from the shore. Before him Massachusetts Bay glittered all the way from Gloucester Harbor in the east to Boston Harbor in the west. We are told that he made up his mind instantly: this land with its great pines and oaks, its wave-thundering craggy shore and the long arc of the horizon should be his domain. He would build his house on this cliff and establish his family here for the long seasons when he was not using the winter house on Beacon Hill. So, although Boston society criticized him for marooning his wife so far away from civilization (Nahant and Lynn being the summer resorts of the 1850s and 60s), he bought parcels of land from neighboring farmers and engaged Van Brunt (already appointed as architect of Harvard's Memorial Hall) to design his house. This turned out to be a Victorian-Gothic castle, complete with porte-cochère, wrought iron flourishes topping elaborate facades framing high gabled windows set into a steep slate roof, and a mysterious tower brandishing an iron banner against the sky.

Let us leave our vehicle under the arches of the porte-cochère, brave the stuffed elk and buffalo heads on the porch's wall, and open the front door. We are immediately aware that we have stepped back into an era of expansiveness, when there was no limit to America's frontiers, when material acquisitions denoted a gentleman's standing, and when waste space was not immoral.

The front hall is big enough to seat a hundred guests for a gala dinner, and its parquet floor to sustain half a hundred waltzing couples at a time. The fireplace rises four yards to the ceiling, with fluted columns of chestnut wood flanking arched niches, above the eight-foot-long mantel-shelf (which is itself six feet above the parquet floor). Tapestries hang on the walls between soaring pilasters, each topped with a Corinthian capital, intricately carved. The living room and dining room, opening from the hall, are also of generous proportions, designed for robust living. And above the vast entrance hall, matching it in size, is the billiard hall, flanked on three sides by bedrooms. When Van Brunt designed this whimsical summer palace, there was only one Curtis child. However, as years rolled on, more and more children arrived. In all, Harriot Curtis bore twelve children, of whom ten lived to maturity. By 1887, a third floor was added above the billiard hall, providing four more bedrooms. Thus, with a little doubling up, there was room for Greely Stevenson Curtis, his wife Harriot Appleton Curtis, their ten children and several servants, as well as a steady stream of visiting relatives and friends.

Family solidarity was still a prevailing element in the America of the last third of the 19th century, and perhaps nowhere better exemplified than by the Curtis family at Manchester. Family cohesion was strong partly because it was customary, but significantly because "Sharksmouth" was almost a self-sufficient world. While its untamed woodlands, sea and rocky shore provided ample space and diversity for ten children, its vegetable garden, orchard and pastures provided most of their food. Aside from such staples as sugar and flour, coffee, tea and Sunday roast beef, food was home-grown, from the lush strawberries of June to the melons and apples, the grapes and quinces of September; from the early peas and lettuce to the last squash and pumpkins. The piglets that fattened all summer became ham and bacon for the winter months. The cows produced gallons of milk and cream; the hens laid so many eggs that dozens were put down in "waterglass" for cooking. And when the hens outlived their laying, they became boiled fowl. Every spring there were new-hatched chicks in the henyard, and in the farm-barn two or three little calves. When the autumn days grew harsh, great logs of timber, felled in the surrounding woods, stoked the furnace of the castle, and smaller ones burned in its many fireplaces.

All this abundance did not appear by magic. Edward Hooper, whose forebears were early Manchester settlers, took care of the estate. Coming as a youth to work on building the Stone House, he stayed on for the next fifty years. Always called "Mr. Hooper," he managed the place with unfailing competence, creativity and modesty. He always had two workmen to assist with the gardening, livestock and forestry. Labor costs were low in the years when shiploads of immigrants were arriving weekly in Boston. In the Stone House, there were three and sometimes four domestic servants living in, and two laundresses that came by day. While Mr. Hooper ran all the outdoor operations on the property, Mrs. Curtis was in charge of the domestic household.

The day began in the house when she came downstairs, wound the clock by the dining room door, and surveyed the breakfast table to see that it was properly prepared. The household staff had been down for hours already, getting the coal stove going again, heating water to be carried upstairs in pitchers for the family's morning ablutions, setting the table for twelve people. Mrs. Curtis, stepping back into the hall, then called "*Break*fast! Billy-Fanny-Elly-Steen-Bella-Harry-Frazier-Jim-Harriot and Margaret! BREAKFAST'S ready!" Down would troop all ten, to sit in ranks of five on each side of the table. Mr. Curtis sat at the eastern end; Mrs. Curtis at the western. A progression of nourishing food then followed: strawberries and cream, porridge, eggs and bacon, toast and muffins, mugs of milk. All but the porridge was home-grown, and the bread was baked in their own kitchen.

At mealtime, "Cut square and eat all" was the stern rule laid down by the paterfamilias, "or else leave the table." It is no wonder that none of the five daughters were wasp-waisted in later life. But it is curious that when the Aunts, many decades later, repeated their father's martial command, a note of pride would still ring in their elderly voices. Why were they proud of having a didactic and imperious father? Did their mother foster this submissive filial attitude? Probably, to some degree; she was eleven years younger than her husband and had married him, a dashing cavalry officer of 33, when she was still a protected young lady, unexposed to the world beyond her family and schoolmates. She thought of her husband as a hero, as is

14

evidenced by a notebook, still extant, full of courageous episodes that she wrote down for her children. Story after story reveals the bravery of Greely Stevenson Curtis, and they are all *true*, she explains, because she heard them from his own lips. Here is one example:

Greely was in an open boat crossing the Strait of Canso between Nova Scotia and Cape Breton. The other passengers were a handful of women and children, and the boat was rowed by several Nova Scotia fishermen. When they were part way across, a violent storm arose, blackening out the further shore. The wind grew stronger and stronger as the storm loomed nearer and nearer. The crew, familiar with Fundy's fierce tides and waves, decided to return to port, and started to turn the boat around. But Greely pulled out his revolver and aimed it at the first rower's head. "Keep going," he said. They did.

With this example of "courage," the Curtis sons had a bewildering model to follow. It certainly is harder to imitate a myth on a pedestal than a man with his feet on the ground. Moreover, besides being a legendary hero, their father was a semi-invalid all his life. Malaria, the disease which had abruptly curtailed his Civil War career, had left him never free of the threat of its recurrence, and his wife guarded his health carefully through all the years the children were growing up. They were told to hush their voices when coming in the front door and nearing "Pa's" study, where he spent many hours alone. He died in 1897, long before any of his grandchildren were born, but the Aunts reminisced about him as they grew older. Besides quoting his martial commands and telling us frequently about his perpetual ill-health, they also told how he could vault over a five-barred gate using only one hand, how he mastered wild weather at the helm of his yacht, and how he loved to ride fast horses. Privately, we nieces wondered how a chronic invalid could do all this and sire twelve children as well. Though it is true, two of these died in infancy, the other ten grew to strapping maturity.

The Aunts were still perpetuating their father's heroic image as late as 1953. That winter, one of their teenage great-nieces dropped in to pay a call on them. She was looking very pretty with an imitation Confederate Army forage cap on her blonde hair. Aunt Bog ordered her out of the house immediately. Ninety years after he resigned from the Union Army and more than half a century after his death, Greely Curtis had been callously insulted.

Portrait of Greely S. Curtis in Civil War regalia.

Greely Stevenson Curtis
c. 1892

Harriot Appleton
c. 1863

Chapter Two

The Parents:

Greely Stevenson Curtis 1830-1897
Harriot Appleton Curtis 1841-1923

Although my grandfather became a somewhat haloed legend posthumously, in reality he had a very active, adventurous life before his marriage to the wealthy Harriot Appleton. One of seven children, Greely Curtis grew up in a modest wooden house on Pinckney Street—Number 9, still standing, surrounded by the usual Beacon Hill brick ones. His father, James Freeman Curtis, had been a teenage midshipman on the *Constitution* in the War of 1812, had fought pirates in the Caribbean, had run a mill in New Hampshire, and had been superintendent of the Boston and Worcester Railroad since its beginning in 1835. ("Tom Thumb," the first steam-powered engine, had made its successful run in 1830.) But James Curtis was killed in a horrible railroad accident in 1839, when Greely was only nine years old. There was very little money, and the seven children were brought up and given lessons at home by their widowed mother and two aunts. One can imagine how often their father was held up before the children as a brave example by these loving women.

When Greely outgrew his aunts' schooling, he went to Boston Latin School. Here he was known for his pranks and daring and made an erratic scholastic record. He was brave, too, for at the risk of his own life, he rescued a drowning boy who had fallen through the ice while skating on the Back Bay, for which he was awarded a gold medal by the Humane Society. After leaving the Latin School, intending to become a civil engineer, he worked as an apprentice on projects in Newton, Nova Scotia and Canada before enrolling in the Scientific School of Harvard in 1851. But he soon gave up his studies here, as he was suffering from "weak eyes," a common complaint in those days. He then signed on as a seaman before the mast on a ship bound for the Mediterranean. In Rome, he climbed the outside of St. Peter's dome; in Venice, "I lolled back in my gondola," he wrote his family, "feeling myself expand as a perfect gentleman, wearing my best yellow kid gloves." Back in Boston that summer, he decided to join his older brother James in California. He left home in October 1852, sailed around the Horn aboard the "Flying Fish," and in late January 1853, he arrived in San Francisco, where his big brother "Jem" (who had come out with the "Forty-niners") kept a store by the harbor. Greely worked in the store off and on for the next two years. His colorful and exuberant letters to his dear family back home in Boston give a lively picture of San Francisco in its infancy.

San Francisco, Feb. 8, 1853

My dear Isa,

I have been travelling round the dusty streets, staring at the mixture of nations with which they are filled, and have at length come home, feeling rather discontented on account of tight boots, and have sat down to write home. The same evening that we came up harbor a boat came off with a note from Jem telling me that all were well at home and that he was waiting for me ashore. So ashore I went with a curious feeling, marched up to his store and there he was, the same Jem that left home four years ago.

This is a curious place, full of bustle and business—also dust. You hear all sorts of languages spoken as you walk the streets from Chinese to Dutch. When I say streets, don't imagine Tremont nor Washington St. but small buildings like—I don't know what to compare them with except the suburbs of some city, the Fremont Road only narrower, muddier, and ten times busier, with groups of Chinese opening their eyes to their greatest littleness, staring at a wax dummy in the barber shop...the native Indians who look like devils but are very harmless, dressed in dirty blankets and patent leather boots, etc., etc. but

20

the best place to get an idea of the mixture of the population is in some great gambling saloon where you hear—Caramba! Sacrre—Cospetto—der tuyfet! Be Jasus! Darn it! in all tones...

I went the other day with Jem about fifty miles up country to the ranch of an old fellow who was a most interesting specimen of a class that I had never seen before. He was raised in Kentucky, a first cousin of old Zach,[1] a frontier man all his life; left Texas because it was too crowded, has been taken prisoner by the Indians three times, all the fingers of his left hand chopped off by a bowie knife, in trying to save a friend's life; a scar on his face, in fact illustrated with cuts to any extent. He came to the city the other day and got into what he called a tantrum, and having been the best shot in his younger days he disliked to back out of a shooting match now that he is 65. So to settle a dispute as to which was the better shot, he fired at and smashed a bottle on the head of his opponent. But when it was the turn of the other Wm. Tell, he fired too low and raked the old general's head fore and aft, leaving an indentation which I could put my finger into. The old fellow didn't wince, but claimed the victory, which was allowed him. With all this he has one of the mildest frankest faces I ever saw. We slept in his ranch, which was the hull of an old ship made fast to the bank of the river and the old fellow gave us his best of everything. When he is down at the city he domesticates himself at Jem's store, whom he likes much; in the winter he shoots game, bears, elk. If old Zach looked like this one, he must have been prepossessing.

...Last Sunday I went to church the first time for some months. The minister was of the German persuasion and gargled out his gutterals to the utter impossibility of understanding him. The church is of wood with stained glass windows. I mention this latter fact to give you some idea of the progress of fine arts in this city. The ladies bonnets looked quite Parisian or Bostonian....I see lots of Boston boys here. I met Geo. Lipton who has been here nearly a year—Jem's friend Dimnold—Howard Cunningham has not yet come—150 days out—but there are lots of ships who have been out 200 days.

[1] Zachary Taylor, 12th U. S. President.

James Freeman Curtis
1825-1915
older brother of Greely,
who visited him in San Francisco

SAN FRANCISCO
"This view of the lay of the ground and the sweep of the bay is very
correct though how much more crowded with shipping and
in fact with buildings. — Respects, GSC."

April 28, 1853

Right opposite our store is an old hulk with a woman for a figure head. The woman's name is Ada. She is an awful object. Whenever I look up from my desk that high intellectual forehead meets my gaze and returns stare for stare. There is something painfully fascinating about her eye; her big wooden optic regards me fixedly and at times drives me almost frantic....

...Dave Cunningham has just come down from the mining country...and gives great accounts of the people. Sunday afternoons it is the custom for those who want a little exercise...to go out and kill the miserable Indians—the Digger tribe are poor wretches who live on worms and roots and are far inferior to any other tribe on this continent.

...There goes a Chinaman, who grins at me in recognition...it is Howard C's servant; he is clothed in celestial garb, excepting the head only, which is surmounted by a low-crowned broadbrimmed California wide-awake, which I well remember as his master's. The Chinese are a funny people; they are all alike, to an unaccustomed eye—like darkeys—but the best sort have a rather contemptuous smile on their lips as if they still consider us as the barbarians.

After a couple of years working for his brother Jem, Greely left San Francisco for the glamorous gold-country to make his fortune.

Potter's Bar, Feather River
March 10, 1855

Dear Mother,

I lost the opportunity of writing to you by the last mail...but I hoped that Jem would mention to you that I had left town. Potters Bar is a settlement consisting of a rough miners store and one cotton (canvas) house perched on a hill with the river flowing in front. The country all around is very mountainous and it being the rainy season, every little brook has become a torrent....Bidwells is the nearest town to us & the place on the Northern route where the stage road stops, all travelling beyond being done by horse and mule. For three days the driver has had to swim his horses and stage across a river much to the horror of the inside passengers....

I am growing more avaricious every day....it will be very exciting in a couple of months, for then we shall be taking out the Oro in large quantities; only think of having so much gold mixed with dirt in a pail that you can't lift it. And taking out of the river $18,000 in 48 hours. Those are the things which we are thinking about.

At the end of the summer, however, Greely came home to Boston, bringing with him his entire fortune in gold—just enough yellow dust to make a wedding ring, eight years later.

Perhaps it was inevitable that Harriot Appleton fell in love with Greely Curtis. She was still a schoolgirl when he returned from the West, a dashing man of twenty-five, eleven years her senior. Young Hattie Appleton, meticulously-raised daughter of widely-esteemed Nathan Appleton, lived at 39 Beacon Street, in the elegant house her father had built opposite the Common. We know that while skating on the Frog Pond in winter afternoons, Greely singled her out from her schoolmates, helped her teetering balance, and towed her around on the ice in an altogether fascinating way. She was captivated by this great grown-up man; his tales of wild adventures, his dramatic ideas and exuberant jokes were a new experience. No wonder her parents were considerably concerned; no wonder Hattie was charmed, if we consider her carefully circumscribed childhood. A glance at her journal, begun when she was eight years old, gives us an idea of how young ladies of Boston were early nurtured in mind, body and spirit. Its first page is embellished with verses by Isaac Watts, D.D., scrupulously penned, with loving attention to squirls and flourishes enhancing capital letters:

A GENERAL SONG OF PRAISE TO GOD

How glorious is our heavenly King
Who reigns above the sky!
How shall a child presume to sing
His dreadful Majesty?
My heart resolves, my tongue obeys;
And angels shall rejoice
To hear their mighty Maker's praise
Sound from a feeble voice.

AGAINST PRIDE IN CLOTHES

Why should our garments, made to hide
Our parents' shame, provoke our pride?
The art of dress did ne'er begin
Till Eve our mother learnt to sin.

March 1st, 1850. This morning after breakfast I wrote some in my journal then read some after that I fixed my baby house after I had fixed it I went into Mamma's room to write a letter to Papa after I came back into the nursery again I tried to finish fixing my baby house by putting on some coals which I had made but it was all in vain so I laid down and cried pretty soon I stopped crying & Sarah fixed up the coals & I sat down to Paint with Willie...

March 3rd. This morning before breakfast I sat down & read some in the testament then I had breakfast after eating which I read until it was time to dress for Church I went to Church with Sarah after Church I drew on my slate until Dinner time after dinner I went to Church with Sarah again after Church I took off my things & went into Mamma's room to tell her that Mrs. Lowell had called then I came back into the nursery & had my supper after which I said my catechism & some hymns & went to bed.

Such were the events in the life of this good little eight-year-old girl. But the following year was more interesting, for Hattie, with her nurse, went abroad that summer to join her parents in England. "What do you think!" she wrote to her little brother Natie from the ship *Canada* on its way to Bristol. "A wonderful thing happened in the dining saloon: a gentleman at the *British* table rose and gave a toast to 'The President of the United States.' Whereupon a gentleman at the *American* table rose and toasted 'The Queen'!! We had blanc-mange for dessert."

November 16, 1853. My 12th birthday. Mamma gave me a beautiful bracelet of her hair with a heart shaped locket hanging from it...Willie gave me a knife with my name on it. Papa gave me a large and beautiful edition of Mrs. Heman's poems with a delightful note.

Hattie Appleton and Grandma Harriot Sumner, 1852

The "delightful note" Papa wrote to his beloved daughter read:

> Dear Hatty. I avail myself of the happy occasion of your twelfth birthday to present to you a volume containing Mrs. Heman's poems. The delicacy, purity and devotion which characterizes these poems will I have no doubt make them favorites with you, and will, I hope, strengthen those qualities in your own character.
>
> *Your affectionate father,*
> *Nathan Appleton*

Harriot Appleton's journal all through her early teens records much piety and introspection. However, in the summer of '58 when she was sixteen, her religious musings and self-incriminations gave way before more pressing affairs. The Appleton family was staying in Lynn, their usual summer resort, when Greely Curtis and his cousin Pelham showed up in the neighborhood.

Lynn, July 15. Friday. Our chief object of interest for the last fortnight has been Mr. Greely Curtis. Adie Bigelow has been staying here, and we have had a good time *rather*. The very first night she was here we got out of my window onto the shed at about midnight in nightgowns and bare feet just to see what it would seem like. Our time has been spent mostly in playing billiards with Mr. G.C., in boating with ditto or in looking forward to or back upon those operations....

...He administered to me yesterday an old article on Teaching and Training....He insists particularly that Education should be training not teaching. That a chief principle is that the Individual is for the State, not the State for the Individual & that there should always be some sort of reference to the people as soldiers.... Education for the lower classes is not to teach them to despise their poverty but to find contentment in it....

Sunday. Greely and Pelham came over in the morning and Pelham talked lightly about keeping Sunday. He said he saw no reason why we shouldn't play billiards on Sunday except common custom. He declared that somebody and Agassiz had disproved Moses' account of the Creation....I had a very nice talk with Greely on the way home from Church. He brings me down deliciously from my vague flights—by saying he dont seem to see it—meaning he sees quite through it. I have rather a habit of making remarks which are meant to sound impressive...and Mr. G. is so practical & so very bright he nips them in the bud.

It is no wonder that Grandmamma, Mrs. Jesse Sumner, felt urged to write Hattie the following note:

I beg you not to venture often in a sailboat with Mr. Curtis or anyone except the good skipper who goes out with parties. You have grown so wild you have even made your little horse so.

Two years later, her parents arranged a visit in New York for Hattie. Here she would stay with friends of theirs and broaden her social horizon. She certainly did. Ah-h, New York in May 1860! And Hattie Appleton, the little Boston heiress, wasp-waisted, hoop-skirted, age eighteen in the spring of life, laughingly ready for every opera, dinner-party and dancing partner that High Society could provide! Hattie's daily letters home to her mother were ecstatic:

Saturday, April 28th

Brother Tom took Lotty and me yesterday to see Rouse, Bierstadt, Church, Gignaux, Haseltine and Suydam. Tonight he takes us to the opera Trovatore. I bought me a bonnet yesterday at Dorsay's, but a horrible thought has seized me that I have forgotten to bring my hair rats, and how can I roll my hair on Monday evening.

Tuesday, May 1st

I went last night to a New York party. A large full dress talk music but no dancing. I had a much better time than I expected. I saw one man who looked like a Bostonian and my discrimination was shown when he turned out to be Sidney Everett and was very good fun. Jimmy Otis is delicious also a Mr. Bridge and Hamilton Hawkins....Jimmy Otis is thought to be the best looking man in New York but I don't think handsome men abound at all.

...I ordered a dress at Deiden's yesterday and I am to wear it tonight at Miss Belden's. Tuesday is a party at the Grinnell's and I shall wear my muslin all trimmed over pink and the high neck cape made low.

Wednesday, May 9th

...What in the world did I write that was of a different style. Why had I better come back. I shant do any such thing. Went with Lotty to a jolly party last night at the Grinnells. We were asked *socially* at 8. We went at quarter of 10 and were the first there and waltzed with Mr. Grinnell and Mr. Schuyler round the almost empty rooms, it was a delight. Everybody waltzes here and when you are in Rome you should do as the Romans do. The gas went out and it was fun.

Thursday, May 10th

Had a jolly time yesterday. Fancy a stately dinner party at Mr. Josiah Lane's cards on peoples plates and every kind of superiority. Behold before your mind's eye your little daughter flounced to the head sweeping in with the old gentleman at the head of the procession. I was between him and Mr. Ehringer and it was first rate fun. They have Roman punch right in the middle of a dinner. Isn't it funny? I of course behaved as if every day of my life had included a dinner made expressly for me. Mr. Ehringer certainly is very far gone. Well no wonder! Afterwards Thomas and I went to a little party....Dr. and Mrs. Bellows were there and Mr. Willis who sang and a lady played. Ah you should see me in that lilac grenadine. Mrs. Gibbs thought it the prettiest dress she had seen this year. I had a nice little flirtation with Joe which was fun. Today we have a dinner party. Tomorrow the opera, next day dine with Georgie Sargent....

Saturday
Dear Marm,
What in the name of common sense did I write to put you in such a state of mind? Was it about Mr. Ehringer. Havent you got used to your daughter yet?...Mr. Ehringer is an elderly amiable artist and a most particular friend of Mr. Hazeltine's, but bless my soul!

It was probably not the doting Mr. Ehringer that upset Mrs. Appleton, but the party at the Grinnells'. Waltzing! In an empty ballroom, with failing lights, her daughter Hattie had been *waltzing*. In Boston, no real lady ever danced the waltz. The polka, and the gavotte, yes; but the waltz required that a gentleman's arm encircle a lady's waist. Hattie came home. When the Prince of Wales visited Boston that autumn of 1860, a great ball was held in his honor. It was carefully arranged beforehand that Miss Appleton should be His Royal Highness's partner in the minuet.

Greely Curtis, meanwhile, had not swerved from his interest in Harriot Appleton, nor she from interest in him. By the time the Civil War began, and Greely had enlisted in the 1st Massachusetts Cavalry, they were virtually engaged. He wrote her regularly, all those months he was in the south, giving her accounts of the battles, skirmishes and forays. But by the summer of 1863, he was so badly disabled by malaria that he came home on sick leave. They were married the following November, and Greely received his honorable discharge after they set off for their prolonged honeymoon in Europe.

Once established on Beacon Hill and at Sharksmouth, Greely and Harriot ruled their growing brood with spirit and devotion. While Greely, as noted earlier, ruled with the austere barks of a general commanding his troops, Harriot gently and pervasively guided her ten children through their childhood years. She became more and more deeply immersed in her children: their lives became hers and remained so, decade after decade, when they were full grown. Though innocent of scheming, and by no means possessive in nature, she gradually wove a net which kept them all in the meshes of Curtis family life. This webbing was greatly strengthened by her propensity for letter-writing. Her constancy in writing to any one of her children who was absent from home was unfailing. Even if one was away for two or three days only, visiting a nearby friend, she would be sure to dash off a letter or a postcard. And of course her children were expected to write back. The girls always did, though the boys were often remiss. Always keeping in touch with home, always having home brought to them by the daily post, no matter how far away they were (be it Egypt, London or simply Milton, Massachusetts) must have been a significant factor in keeping the girls away from marriage. No daughter really had much chance to discover her personal self as an individual young woman with sensitivities, wishes and reactions all her own. All was put into the family melting pot; all was tinted with familial coloring, in the letters that plied back and forth. Fanny, the eldest daughter, was perhaps the most reliable of her mother's correspondents. Visiting friends in Richmond when she was in her twenties, she writes, "I arrived just ten minutes ago and haven't unpacked my valise yet, thinking I'd dash you a line first." And when the Curtis parents were off on one of their rare trips, it was usually Fan who answered her mother's anxious inquiries about family doings at home.

Dear Lady, I am inheriting your powers of correspondence. Hal has not bought his coat, Jim has won his football fame. Peg has learned her spelling lesson. El and Bel have come back from their calls....To the mail—your attached daughter.

(P.S.) Don't you think I have caught your style quite successfully and particularly as it is just ten minutes before eight?...All are well and good.

Elinor, however, sends her a livelier description of the growing family:

> Ted writes. Jib sprawls in a big chair and annoys kind sister Frang [Frances] by flippant comment on her endeavors to have him read serious works....Jib has now gone back to Emerson and Ted wants to know if that scene in the barroom isn't inimitable and nearly up to "Three Men in a Boat." Writing under these circumstances is a good deal of a chore—for of course neither of those children is silent for more than ten consecutive seconds....

And here is what young Ted (Frazier) was writing his mother at that very moment:

> We've been having a doos of discussion this evening. First Frang started to read aloud Browning, but I dodged that by hiding it under my breeks, sitting on it, while it lay perdu in my chair. Then she grasped poor little Apes by the collar and thrust a volume of Emerson down his gullet. The puny little varmint whimpers that he has read Everybody's Column in the paper, but no, stern sister will have it. Berry [Elinor] meanwhile sits by and wheezes in a manner, as Jib and I both agree, which is extremely offensive to all right thinking persons. Frang froths at the mouth when I ask Ape if he has gitted to the dog fight in chapter two, and says that she, for one read and appreciated Emerson when she was 15 and that she considers Ape o' Ninetails a singularly ignorant young person.
>
> Yes, Miss Milbury is coming to the Sturgises. Yes, Frang brought into the house a copy of the Folly of Ren Harrington. Yes Frang hides stamps in a singularly disagreeable manner. Even Jib, hardened cynic that he is, noticed and commented on it unfavorably. Frang feels pretty badly, but continues sawing wood. She is a splendid child....

No wonder that Frazier Curtis, this verbal acrobat at 14, became editor of the *Harvard Lampoon* a few years later!

William Curtis (Billy)
(1865-1898)

James F. Curtis (Jibby)
(1879-1952)

Frazier Curtis (Teddy)
(1877-1940)

The Uncles
c. 1894

Greely S. Curtis Jr. (Steen)
(1871-1947)

Harry A. Curtis (Harry)
(1875-1966)

Chapter Three

The Uncles

Although the boys and girls grew up together, raised under the same parental precepts, sharing a close and lively family childhood, as adults the brothers had more difficulty than their sisters in becoming self-reliant, effective individuals. Surrounded by plenty, with a father who had no professional ambition and a mother who made a hero of him, it is remarkable that the brothers succeeded as well as they did in the world beyond the family domain. Two of them, indeed, had considerable success in their personal careers. Except for Billy, they all graduated from Harvard, and all married, though only two produced families of their own. Billy, the oldest, was mentally handicapped from birth and took his own life when still young.

The next oldest son was Greely Stevenson Curtis, Jr., always called "Steen," or "Stivets," by his family. He was born in 1871, and soon began to show ingenuity and an inventive mind. After the Lilienthal brothers, early explorers of aerodynamics, visited America to demonstrate their successful glider, young Greely, along with many other Americans, was vastly impressed. Absorbed with the idea that man might actually be able to fly, he started experimenting. After graduating from Harvard in 1892 he planned to study aeronautics with the Lilienthals, in Zurich. His father, however, flatly forbade him to go. Greely Senior knew for sure that man would never fly, and therefore his son's desire was an adolescent pipe dream, something to get over as soon as possible. He made Steen go to Cornell, allowing him to study electrical engineering, however, for work on solid ground. While Steen was at Cornell, his mother wrote him almost every other day, three or four pages of home news: the social doings of his sisters...why not come home for our dinner party on the

27th...Harry's struggles with exams...the dog's adventure on Boston Common. But sometimes she was also admonitory:

> Now dont overwork yourself with your 10 or 12 hours of advanced electrical laboratory daily, for when you get tired you have jaundice or boils or something....And dont go flying in any of your machines for you might get killed. I told your father I would not show him your last letter as it was full of flying machinery and he accepted that view at once, and didnt want to see it. He puts it all in the same category as the Elixir of Life, the Philosopher's Stone & Perpetual Motion.

Steen stayed at Cornell for three years. During that time he never wavered from his purpose of ultimately inventing a flying machine, and he was determined to join the Lilienthals in Zurich, the autumn of 1894, to develop his invention further. His parents were still trying to blunt his ambition, however. During his last semester at Cornell, his mother wrote him more subtly than before:

> I keep thinking of what you are to do when you go abroad. I suppose the old scheme of studying at the Zurich school would not be much use now, so far as electrical learning goes. You must have acquired all they have to teach except the language—and in that condition of things how can you decide what you had better do? Your father thought of letting you take Billy over with you giving him a few weeks with you, then you could just put him on a steamer at Bremen when you should begin to settle down to study German somewhere....

Steen was not to be dissuaded this time. After the summer at home to placate his parents, he sailed to Europe for serious work with the Lilienthals on aeroplane design. During the next three years, his absorbing work in Zurich was only interrupted for a few short vacations spent escorting his sisters through the Alps, in Italy, and up the Nile. His parents of course felt that taking care of his sisters and having a good time among great cultural sights was far more worthwhile than pursuing a totally worthless dream.

At the time the Wright brothers made their amazing flight at Kitty Hawk in 1903, there were quite a few other eager aeronautical engineers designing planes. One of these was Starling Burgess of Marblehead. He and Steen formed a company,—Burgess Company and Curtis—and set up an airplane factory in Marblehead. In those early years of aviation, there were "flying meets." For these air-shows, aviators were hired who gave hair-raising demonstrations in a variety of newly-invented planes. Mrs. Curtis (now a widow, and reconciled to her son Steen's career) remarked in one letter that "Steen is looking hard for a good aviator for the Long Island Meet next month. The good ones come high—but unfortunately the less expensive ones are apt to come tumbling down." Lots of them *did* fall down, of course, and a newspaper clipping of Steen (who was an "Early Bird" flier) has a picture of him, standing safe and sound on Plum Island, with his crumpled plane hanging limply from a tree above.

The
Burgess Company
and Curtis

Will take pleasure in showing you the latest types of

Burgess Model A

Burgess Model D

SINGLE-PASSENGER AND TWO-PASSENGER
BURGESS BIPLANES
which will be exhibited from

February 20 to February 25 at the Second National Exhibition of Aerial Craft
Mechanics Building, Boston, Mass.

The exhibit will include the veteran "Flying Fish" and the No. 10 with its record of three-passenger flights, as well as the latest "Grahame-White Biplane," ordered by Mr. C. Grahame-White, a duplicate of which Mr. Grahame-White is now flying in England

W. STARLING BURGESS.
GREELY S. CURTIS.

Marblehead, Mass., February, 1911

During World War I, Burgess and Curtis built planes for England's newly-created Air Force. The Tsar of Russia was also interested and sent an emissary to the factory in Marblehead. The Wright brothers were also curious. A postcard of Mrs. Curtis to one of her children reads: "Steen has Orville Wright on his hands for the weekend, and wants to bring him over. I suppose they've got to stay for dinner." All through the war years Burgess and Curtis flourished, but on November 11, 1918, the factory caught fire. It was Armistice Day, and all the sirens and churchbells of Marblehead and Salem were ringing, while rockets and fireworks shot into the sky. Everyone thought the shooting flames and screaming siren of the factory were just part of the joyous celebration of Peace. The factory was a total loss and all it contained a heap of ashes. Burgess & Curtis was ruined. With this disaster, Steen's public career came to an end. After that, he busied himself with ingenious home inventions, with handling the financial affairs of his sisters and the Manchester estate, and with serving as trustee of diverse good causes. He was also a senior warden of King's Chapel in Boston.

Steen was the reliable brother the family all counted on. Ever since his father's death in 1897, he had taken care of his mother's financial affairs, meting out funds for her household and allowances for his younger brothers. As they grew older, he usually bowed to his mother's pleas that her younger sons' adventurous schemes be funded. Yes, Steen was the one they all relied on for his measured judgment, exactness to the point of minisculity, and his fairness.

Harry Appleton Curtis, the next in age (after Billy, Fanny, Elly, Steen and Bella) was about as different from Steen as any two brothers can be. Where Steen was prudent, Harry was extravagant; while Steen moved worthily among conscientious board members of Boston charities, Harry moved dashingly among the showiest members of New York Society. Harry was considered the handsomest of the Curtis boys, the tallest, with blue eyes and an ever-ready smile. Because his chin receded, his brothers and sisters called him "Chinny," a nickname that stuck by him through life.

The earliest record of Harry still extant is a memorandum he wrote for himself when he was seven years old, and which his doting mother preserved under the title of "Harry's Plans 1882":

> Go and get 2 cent worth of Marbls.
> Save up Muny an bie a Verlosapeed
> Practis the now way of snaping
>
> H A C

The note is a prophecy of Harry's days to follow. The new way

way of snapping one's fingers was doubtless an important social asset among seven-year-olds; and as for money—well, you can't really have a good time living-it-up without it.

Harry got through Harvard just in time to join Teddy Roosevelt's Rough Riders in the Spanish-American War, then went west, where mines were opening up in Colorado. For a few weeks he studied engineering in Denver, before taking on the job of mine supervisor in a prolific vein nearby. From Cripple Creek he wrote his mother that life was wonderful and he planned to enjoy it to the full. After elk hunting in the Tetons,. and beauing around the pretty daughters of mining magnates in Denver, he returned to the east. For a brief moment he thought he might be a newspaper reporter covering the construction of the Panama Canal—if someone in the family knew someone who could get him the job. Well, what did it matter? Life was still wonderful.

Harry lived in New York for most of his life. With an assured and ample income as Chief Electrical Engineer for the St. Regis Hotel (a position he didn't exactly qualify for, but a friend had gotten him the job) he lived exuberantly. He had his own personal bootlegger during the Prohibition years; he was a favorite at the Tennis and Racket Club where he gambled for high stakes at backgammon with merry insouciance. He married Grace Fargo, granddaughter of the pioneer of the Wells-Fargo Express. She was beautiful and gentle, and her picture appeared several times in *Vogue* and the rotogravure section of the *New York Times* among the Best-Dressed Women of America. But she was frail, and the childless marriage ended with her death after a few years.

Harry continued to be charming, handsome, and beloved by all—by his rich high-stepping cronies in New York and by his sisters, who made much of him whenever he showed up at Manchester. Though they heartily disapproved of his way of life with his gambling and drinking friends, they rushed to the door in their uncouth shabby clothes when his sleek Cadillac convertible whisperingly arrived and his Japanese valet sprang out to take care of the luggage. We nieces also loved Uncle Harry. He joked and laughed with us, treating us as people (not just children) and giving us a glimpse of a glittering world beyond our simple life at Manchester. Always carefree with his money, whether getting or spending, he gave magnificent presents, too: an elegant bicycle to a particularly pretty niece, a diamond and platinum watch to his favorite sister.

But age caught up with him too soon, bringing crippling arthritis to subdue that carefree spirit. I have a vivid memory of Uncle Harry visiting my parents—a last visit, as it turned out to be. My father and mother were teaching each other to play Chinese Checkers, a new instrument for their mutual enjoyment which had already lasted for forty years. Harry tottered across the room on his two canes and settled in a chair near them. He sat and looked with puzzled eyes and a friendly eagerness to understand at my unworldly father, who never drank, gambled or swore, was fifteen years his senior but still nimble and lithe, full of pleasure in simple things, full of puritan principles. I had always thought of my father as a humble man, but this time my heart went out to Uncle Harry.

When Harry Curtis died, he left the bulk of his estate to Miss X, the woman "who taught me how to drink." This legacy fits in well with his philosophy, his generosity, easy giving, easy taking, laughter and charm. He took life as it came, probably never thinking there was much he could contribute beyond good fellowship. "*Dear* Harry" was about all Mother said, after that last visit of his.

Frazier (called "Frère" or "Teddy") was the fourth son and seventh child in the Curtis family. Full of athletic pranks, and verbal ones as well, he kept his brothers and sisters laughing much of the time. He had an amazing vocabulary and a wonderful capacity for calling objects and people by sly misnomers, and though these were often a bit off the beam, everybody found him delightfully funny.

At Harvard, he became well-known for his wit. Not only was he editor of the *Lampoon*, but he also wrote the script of the Hasty Pudding show of 1898. This was a rollicking and savage spoof of the Spanish-American War, going on at the time. The show was a hit, and rated special attention in the Boston newspapers.

Following graduation, he plunged enthusiastically into one career after another. At first, raising beef-cattle in Cuba was going to be his life work. He wrote his mother from Cuba that he would need a lot of money to begin with, because of course he'd have to go to Texas to *get* the cattle, and then shipping them to Cuba would be expensive. Next, the Klondike Gold Rush had him enthralled, and he set off for the West Coast. No gold fell into his hands, so he turned again to cattle-ranching, this time in the west. When the life of a rancher began to seem rather drab, he realized that what he *really* wanted to do was make a fortune in coast-wise shipping between Puget Sound and California. He already had his eye on a beautiful schooner (he wrote his mother) which would do very well for a start. And of course the money needed to set up this coast-wise trade with ships would all come back to the family, once the enterprise became the great success it was bound to be.

Early in his western travels, Frazier met an English girl on a train. They started talking, and after the train trip was over, they started writing. They never met again until after they had agreed—by letter—to be married. When Frazier wrote his family telling that Gladys Raper, his fiancée, was coming east to Boston, and wanted to meet them, there was considerable apprehension. Was this another of Frère's erratic enthusiasms? Was this going to be a passing fancy? A cheap little gold-digger, maybe?

Not at all! Gladys Raper came to tea at "Twenty-Eight," where the family was assembled. Almost six feet tall, this strapping, handsome, pink-cheeked girl from Battle, England, won the hearts of all. She was healthy and athletic; she was humorous and warm-hearted; she was full of common sense. Frazier and Gladys were married at Manchester that summer of 1909.

What a magical person Aunt Gladys was! After she and Uncle Teddy returned to Manchester from World War I (and before they moved to California), we children spent as much time as possible with her. She had spent the war years cheering British tommies in a canteen near the Front. She taught us lots of their favorite songs—"Its a long way to Tipperary..." "Anybody here seen Rover?" "Heigh Ho! Cant ya hear the Steamer? Heigh Ho...." She also played wonderful ragtime on the piano ("Everybody's Doing It—doing what? Turkey Trot..."). We little girls followed her around everywhere, hanging on her elbows—and her every word.

As the years passed, Gladys's strength of spirit was much needed by Frazier. The whimsy, wild witticisms and fantastic imagination with which he had delighted everyone as a boy became more pronounced and rather sinister when he was a man. In World War I, he joined the Lafayette Escadrille. One story has it that he was shot down in flames; another that he was merely grounded by his superior officer. Whatever the facts, when he returned he appeared to be so mentally deranged that his family put him in a sanitarium. Gladys soon took him out, and they moved to La Jolla, California. Here she took care of him for the rest of his tormented life. She laughed with him, soothed his phobias, tolerated his strange beliefs and cravings with unfailing sympathy. Gladys's ebullience, humor and ever-generous view of life were magnetic, and she made many good friends in La Jolla. But Frazier, in spite of her steadfast devotion, year after year became more estranged from reality and one evening in 1940, when Gladys had gone to bed, he told her he'd take a stroll before joining her. Gladys found his body the next morning, near the front door. After his death, she continued to live in La Jolla, and wrote cheerful and delightful letters to her sisters-in-law from time to time, and they kept up with her, often sending along some money (for Uncle Teddy had never earned any). During World War II she worked in a munitions factory in San Diego—on the night shift. She was well over sixty by that time, but nothing ever stopped that dauntless woman.

Gladys was the only one of their sisters-in-law that the Aunts approved. Steen's wife Fanny, when a bride, had been trustingly open and affectionate, but later sat silent and ignored through the obligatory Sunday dinners she endured at Sharksmouth.

40

Harry's wife Grace was too fashionably clothed to join in Manchester activities, which usually called for well-worn saggy skirts and scruffy sneakers. As for Jim's wife Laura, the Aunts flatly disliked her and did not hesitate to say so. Their mother may have been largely responsible for their attitude. Many of her letters to one or another of her daughters include a sly joke or not-altogether-flattering comment about a wife of one of her sons. She was likely unaware that fundamentally she felt the wives were intrusions, extraneous to Curtis family life.

James Freeman Curtis, the youngest of the Curtis sons, was the most successful in the world outside the family. "Uncle Jibby" to us, "Jim," "Jib" or "Jumbo" to his siblings, he was the one son of Greely Curtis who made consistent use of the intellect with which he was endowed and the privileges to which he was born. Graduating from Harvard in 1899 at the age of 21, he immediately went to Law School, where he did brilliantly, and soon thereafter was made a district attorney—the youngest ever to hold this position in the Commonwealth of Massachusetts. After three years as Assistant Attorney-General of Massachusetts, he went to Washington to assume the post of Assistant Secretary of the Treasury. In this position he was instrumental in shaping the newly conceived Federal Reserve System and also took charge of reforming the U.S. Customs Service. The reform bill he devised called for the elimination of a number of official Collectors of Customs. As these were mostly political appointees, Jim ran into trouble with a number of senators, but the reform bill finally passed in 1913, after President Wilson had succeeded William Howard Taft, its instigator.

From 1914 to 1919, James F. Curtis was Counsel, Secretary and Deputy Governor of the Federal Reserve Bank of New York. He then went into private law practice, forming a partnership which became very successful. The New York firm of Curtis, Fosdick and Belknap handled the legal affairs of such clients as the Rockefeller Foundation and its Medical Institute, and the Williamsburg Foundation. Jim Curtis and Fosdick helped organize the Brookings Institution, and both later served on its executive committee.

Financially, Jim Curtis flourished all through the 1920s. Before the great crash of '29 he was a millionaire ten times over, and though his fortune was considerably reduced by 1931, his interests and activities were by no means curtailed. He was well-known and much sought-after for his wide knowledge, sound judgment, keen wit and generous spirit.

But his domestic life became a disaster. Early in his career as Assistant Secretary of the Treasury, he had met Laura Merriam, the beautiful blonde daughter of the Governor of Minnesota and the belle of Washington Society. Their small home wedding in 1912 was attended by President Taft, the Secretary of the Treasury and the Attorney General, and all the newspapers wrote long and glamorous accounts of the event. But their marriage, after a serene beginning, became increasingly stormy. Despite their three beautiful children and a bounteous estate on Long Island, their relationship foundered, and they were divorced. After a few years of separation, they remarried. Laura soon produced another child, but their mutual antagonism started up again, and they were divorced a second time. Laura then returned to Washington, where she became hostess of a fashionable club, a dining and socializing mecca for many prominent senators and other well-known Washington personalities.

After this, Jim Curtis changed his way of life. Telling his law firm he would work eight months of the year only, he deliberately set out to explore the world beyond his personal entanglements. He had a series of adventures. He went to the Galapagos archipelago with William Beebe; he hunted for Lawrence of Arabia all over the Middle East—only to track down "Aircraftsman Shaw" in Plymouth, England, the night before sailing for home; he hob-nobbed with Douglas Fairbanks (Sr.) in Angkor and with Governor Dwight Davis in the Philippines; he persuaded the president of the Dutch airline KLM to let him be its first passenger to fly from Java to Holland.

In New York, he became increasingly interested in music. He not only went to concerts, but came to know musicians and a good deal about the rigorous training requisite to becoming a successful virtuoso on the concert stage. Jascha Heifetz was a good friend of his, and with this great violinist as his guide, Jim Curtis became both friend and benefactor of a number of young aspiring musicians who were rich in talent but lacked the funds to further their training.

In 1938 he met and married Eleanor Greene, a quiet, loving woman with both feet on the ground. This marriage proved exactly right for both, and at last Jim Curtis knew real domestic happiness. But World War II brought overwhelming tragedy to him: both his sons were killed during Air Force training exercises. I never saw Uncle Jibby smile again. He continued, however, to be wise, observant and supportive to all whom he felt he could help. And thank goodness he had, for the last twenty years of his life, a devoted wife who stood by him through tragedy and failing health until the end. Uncle Jibby was certainly outstanding, both as a friend to many, and as a wise, effective public citizen.

Aunt Fan in her coming-out bonnet
c. 1886

Chapter Four

Aunt Fan

Frances Greely Curtis 1867-1957

Long before "Women's Liberation" became a cause, my Curtis aunts were liberated. Although these four unmarried sisters lived together always in their original home surroundings, and their lives were closely interwoven, each was a very positive and idiosyncratic individual. They all were vitally interested in the world beyond their own household, and three of them took active and effective part in civic and political affairs.

Aunt Fan, the oldest, was born in 1867. She started early on her responsibilities as family manager, for we find her at the age of twelve writing to her temporarily absent parents a report on the doings of all her younger siblings: who was reading "Children of the New Forest," who was taking a walk with the nurse on the Common, who had been snuffling last night but was better now.

Three years later, we get a glimpse of a rather formal father-daughter relationship in a note she wrote from Naushon Island, where she and her sister Elly were visiting: "Dear Papa, At the risk of incurring your displeasure, we shall not be returning on Monday, as previously arranged, but on Tuesday morning, since this is more convenient for the Forbes family. We shall not be travelling unescorted on either the train from Woodshole to Boston or the 1:15 to Manchester. Your affectionate daughter, Fanny."

In 1886, when Fan was nineteen, she and Elly went abroad with Papa, and had a wonderful time in Paris, buying clothes and going to the theater. "Papa complains that we should attend to other subjects in Paris besides dressmaking....Elly has just purchased the very latest fashion of bustle, and it goes very well beneath her new dress...."

During her early twenties, Fanny spent her time like other young ladies in Boston society, dashing from lunch-party to tea, from tea party to dinner party to theatre, day after day, week after week. She enjoyed this immensely. But frivolity was not the only pursuit of young Bostonian ladies. Fanny set up a community centre and library for Negroes on Phillips Street on Beacon Hill. When she discovered that very few of the adults as well as children, knew how to read, she established reading classes, too. She also worked with the Associated Charities of Boston during her twenties, while her sister Elly (my mother) began her life-long commitment to the Children's Aid Society. Fanny's next concern was plumbing conditions on the north side of Beacon Hill, to which newly-arrived families of Italian immigrants were flocking. She went to the State House to propose improvements to the Legislature. When her proposal was turned down, she took a course in sanitary engineering at the Boston Technical School, the predecessor of M.I.T. When she returned again to the Legislature, her revised plan was approved, and the plumbing on Beacon Hill was renovated.

Meanwhile, she continued to keep a responsible eye on her brothers and sisters and gradually took on more and more of the household management of 28 Mt. Vernon Street. Elly and Bella, the sisters nearest to her in age, were her constant companions, but the younger ones were quite troublesome, as seen in a letter of 1893. Her mother was in Chicago at the World Fair; Fan writes her that Harry is paying no attention to his schoolwork, and Pud and Peg (the two littlest girls) were bickering a good deal of the time.

In 1896, Fanny was abroad for most of the year. Taking trips to Europe was considered a good thing, highly approved of by both parents. All through the 1890s and early 1900s there was scarcely a summer when two or three Curtises were not abroad. All good Bostonians were uplifting themselves with European culture; Fan's, Elly's and Bella's letters are redolent with delightful rendezvous in Vevey, Rome and Cairo, in Venice, London, and Madrid, with Cabots, Lowells, Longfellows. Half the fun seemed to be meeting other Bostonians in amazingly historic places. But the 1896 trip was not for pure pleasure only. The Curtis parents were anxious to lure Steen away from his aeronautic obsession and his experiments with the Lilienthal brothers in Zurich. What better idea than getting him to escort his sisters Fan and Bella on a trip down the Nile? This took a deal of persuading. A dozen letters plied to and fro across the Atlantic between Boston and Zurich before it was arranged that he should meet them in Rome, in December 1895. Steen was not the parents' only concern. Bella had become increasingly inflicted with headaches and sleeplessness, and the family as well as the doctor felt a trip abroad, with a complete change of scenery, might be the perfect cure. Since Fanny and Bella were close and sympathetic friends, Fan, with all her energy and enthusiasm, could get Bella busy with interests outside her physical ailments. Indeed she did! They had a wonderful time on the Nile trip (where several fascinating men were also passengers) and later, in England, at the height of the London season. Meanwhile, back at home, their sister Elly was writing them twice a week about what was going on in Boston. Her letters, usually six pages long, are aglow with descriptions of dinner-parties, opera evenings, charming and witty dancing partners. One letter is headed DO NOT READ ALOUD, because it tells that Lucy, Mamie, and Clara (all recently married friends of theirs) are expecting babies by next summer. If Steen is still traveling with his sisters, he shouldn't hear this delicate news. Another letter describes a moonlit sleigh-ride from Beacon Hill to Milton, everybody crammed in in evening clothes, to attend a dance given by Edith Forbes. It was a wonderful party, but the sleigh did not appear to take them home again at the appointed time, so everyone who was stranded played Puss-in-the-Corner in the stable—just as much fun as the dance itself; and when the miscreant sleigh returned, there followed another beautiful hour gliding over the well-packed snow under the full moon, back to Boston.

Fan did not envy Elly's joyful whirling in the social season of

Boston, for she and Bella were no less active in London. At first, their social life depended on the generous hospitality of some English cousins who provided them with dinner parties and sightseeing expeditions; but they thirsted for more regal glamour. On the date of "The Drawing Room" they stood outside Buckingham Palace to watch the Company arriving: "We have assisted at it thoroughly," a letter reports, "from listening to the band play 'America' as the Princess of Wales drove into the Palace yard in her golden coach with four footmen standing up at the back, to admiring the fat coachmen of sundry ambassadors looking exactly like the fat ones in Cinderella. The footmen were beautiful in white silk stockings—and such calves! Staves in claw, powdered hair and cocked hat. Red and yellow trimmed with gold was the favorite livery. The presented ones didn't look very pretty but *such* jewels. Diamond coronets and pearl necklaces...."

Fanny by this time had developed her managerial talents quite successfully. Bella's headaches having been vanquished by the delights of London, Fanny could now focus more freely on her own ambitions. Her manipulative skill was particularly useful when she got wind of an upcoming soirée, to be attended by most of the British nobility, crowned heads and leading parliamentary notables. Following her usual cheerful philosophy that no obstacle is insurmountable, Fanny thought of a way for the Misses Curtis to attend this magnificent event. She wrote a note to a prominent countess:

> Dear Lady _____:
> Although I have not the pleasure of your acquaintance, I write you because I believe we have a mutual friend in Mary Norton. My sister Isabella and I are in London for a few weeks and we hoped to spend some time with Mary—but unfortunately we do not have her address. Is there a chance that she is presently in London, and that you know where we can find her? I don't want to prey upon your kind heart—but if you can help us, we shall be most grateful.

Sure enough, it worked! The next morning a footman delivered a note for the Curtis sisters, inviting them to tea that very afternoon. Of course they went, and of course an invitation to the illustrious ball soon followed. "Not at all pushy, is she," was Bella's comment in her next letter home.

The ball was magnificent, crowded with earls in kneebritches and countesses in coronets. "Dear Joey" [Prime Minister Joseph] Chamberlain was there, with his American wife and sons, and took some time to talk with the Prince of Wales (who apparently looked rather like a stuck pig, surrounded by politely chattering nobility).

The Curtis sisters' thirst for high life continued throughout the London Season, sated by elegant dinner parties and tea in Downing Street with the Chancellor of the Exchequer and Mrs. Harcourt, although, alas, Lord Balfour did not appear. They finished the season with tea on the terrace of the House of Lords with the Honorable Joseph Chamberlain:

> The observed of all observed, we sat and had tea—delicious strawberries—and a very amusing time, as Joey pointed out all the notables. A laughing and important Col. Lockwood joined us—also Mr. Broderick (Under Sec. for War)...Mr. Chamberlain pulled out a "Private and Confidential" Dispatch from Cecil Rhodes, which he read to us—a humorous account of how he'd been made a colonel of a column and hated being "in front to be shot at by the horrid Matabele and their beastly elephant guns that make so much noise." Imagine anyone sympathizing and agreeing with Rhodes—yet here they all do.

During all these weeks of gaiety, Isabella's headaches were not entirely forgotten. How could they be, when almost every letter from Mother contained an anxious inquiry about Bella's head, and how she was sleeping? There were numerous visits to various doctors specializing in headaches, and after each visit, Fanny wrote a reassuring letter to Mother that this specialist really seemed to be on the path to the perfect cure.

Fanny and Isabella came home to Manchester in mid-summer, laden with London-tailored riding habits, golf clubs and dozens of pairs of gloves for the stay-at-homes, as well as gold chains set with occasional pearls.

Back in America, Fanny started again on her customary

summertime round of visits, staying with old friends in New Hampshire, cruising down the Maine coast with others, joining an annually held houseparty in the Adirondacks at Putnam Camp. Her summers almost always included a fortnight's stay with the H. L. Higginsons at Westport, on Lake Champlain. "Uncle Henry" and she were very compatible, and there were often other interesting visitors staying with the Higginsons as well.

It was at Westport that she met Henry Warner two years later, in the summer of 1898. Five years before, Fanny had considered marrying Ted Cabot. Remarkably, a little note from him remained in her desk long after her death: "Dear Fanny: What I told you last July is exactly the same now. I have tried to look at it differently, it is impossible. The hope will return...." Now, at Westport, five years later, she wrote her mother that a very pleasant Mr. Warner was also visiting the Higginsons. In her next letter (mind you, she wrote her mother every day), she remarks that Mr. Warner is an excellent conversationalist, and in her third letter she tells of his recent loss of both wife and only child and how courageously he has faced this: "With what remarkable strength and humility of spirit he has accepted his tragedy, taking up daily life again, and contributing to the community interests about him."

Though I, her niece, never heard Aunt Fan mention his name, nor any of the other aunts ever refer to him during a half-century of close companionship with them, it seems likely that her experience with Henry Warner was a significant episode and possibly a major turning point in Fanny Curtis's life. That winter, following their meeting, he came almost daily to see her at 28 Mount Vernon Streeet, and on days that he was unable to come, he sent her flowers. Of course everyone in the household knew of his devotion, and it was doubtless the topic of much supper-table conversation. Among the hundreds of letters the Aunts never threw away there are plenty referring to H. Warner— though none written by him are to be found. During March 1899, Isabella was off visiting in California, and Fanny wrote her thus:

Lutie gives me lectures on good behavior every morning on her way downstairs, and the advantages of happy marriages. Heavens! Who so ready as I to agree to all that? All these good people can't do better than say do it, do it; without ever showing one *How*.

Without showing her how? Oh poor Aunt Fan! I wonder more and more about the upbringing of those Curtis children. But there was probably more than one reason why the sisters particularly did not know how to express their feelings, or, indeed, recognize that they had emotions at all. For one thing, they grew up in an era when people looked on nature very differently from the present, post-Freudian view. Women's bodies were disguised by tightly-corseted wasp waists and bulged out behind with bustles under their skirts. Simple landscapes hanging on parlor walls were swamped by elaborate huge gold frames; and the parlor was cut off from nature outdoors by heavy curtains, extravagantly draped around the windows. Silverware on the dinner-table (itself clothed in damask) was ponderously lumpy with intricate scrolls, and armchairs were fringed. Were these all expressive of an era when nature had to be covered up for the sake of decency? However, it is obvious that the Curtis parents felt it was far healthier for children to *do things together* than to do things alone, which might lead to introspection. This parental precept was quite likely influential throughout their daughters' lives. Certainly they busied themselves, decade after decade, in good works, lively sports, and games, and they would have considered it a waste of time to consult their personal feelings about these activities. [1]

---

[1] An example of their suppression of emotions occurred in the 1930s. Aunt Hat had been working as Dean of Women at Hampton Institute for four years and at last was coming home for good. The other aunts were obviously delighted. I was spending the evening with them, at Manchester, while Aunt Fan and Aunt Bog were awaiting Aunt Hat's return. Aunt Pedge had driven up to the South Station to meet her, but the evening wore on and on, and Aunts Fan and Bog fidgeted restlessly, unable to settle down to any conversation or occupation. At last we heard the sound of the car, and we all rushed out to the front porch to meet the home-comer. Sure enough, there was Hat, home at last, sitting

There must have been other reasons why Aunt Fan never married Harry Warner (or Ted Cabot, for that matter). After all, plenty of girls got married in that era of muffling nature in furbelows; and the parental precept that children should do things as a group rather than occupy themselves individually did not prevent the Curtis sons from setting out on disparate careers after college. Did the Curtis parents love each other? Was there ever any manifestation of affection seen by the children? Did Greely ever compliment Harriot, tell her she looked lovely this morning, when they all sat at breakfast together? Of course "sex" was never mentioned in that Victorian age, but if they really enjoyed conjugal life, wouldn't the children have absorbed some signs of it? Or did Harriot, who underwent twelve pregnancies, really fear Greely, covering her aversion with propriety and loyalty to the institution of marriage? I wonder why, in the myriad of letters Mama wrote to her children, she so seldom mentions Papa. There are other indications, too. Decades

---

in the front seat with a big bunch of rhododendrons in her arms that she had carried all the way from Virginia. "Well, I guess it's time these got into water," said Aunt Fan, taking the bunch from her. That was the only greeting Aunt Hat got. They all four walked single file into the house.

At a later time, this habitual failure to recognize personal emotions was almost fatal. Aunt Hat, seriously injured in an automobile accident, was in the hospital in an almost moribund condition, scarcely able to breathe because of broken ribs. After three days she showed no signs of recovery. By the fourth morning, when Aunt Pedge returned from visiting her in the hospital, I asked, "Is she any better?" "No," said Aunt Pedge, "Nothing different....D'you know, I have half a mind to call Jack Gibbon in Philadelphia this evening, after the Long-Distance rates go down." Jack Gibbon was her nephew-in-law, a leading thoracic surgeon, and inventor of the heart-lung machine. "Aunt Pedge," said I, "Why don't you call him right now? It will only cost a dollar or two more. He might be able to fly up this afternoon." I said no more, but waited. After pondering a while, she picked up the telephone and put through the call. It must have taken her some twenty minutes to face the fact that her dearest sister and companion of sixty years was very close to death. Jack Gibbon did come that afternoon, drove immediately to the Beverly Hospital, discovered the jagged rib penetrating the lungs, and Aunt Hat was restored to life.

later, when Aunt Fan, in her eighties, sat darning in her living room, I was browsing through a bookcase nearby. I was fascinated to find among the old favorites of their childhood many volumes in which Mother Curtis had written "SKIP," in her neat handwriting at the top of a page. Some twenty or thirty pages later, there was another notation: "BEGIN AGAIN HERE."

"Aunt Fan, did you all really skip the parts in books that your mother told you not to read?" I asked. "Certainly, my dear," Aunt Fan replied. "Our mother always read books first, before we did, and marked off the disagreeable parts that didn't need to be read." "Were these parts mostly about man-woman sort of stuff?" (I put this question rather vaguely, not wanting to offend her.) "Yes, that. And also any mention of bloodshed. Poor little Jibby used to faint at the sight of blood."

Another time she was reminiscing about swimming: "Of course, we brothers and sisters never went bathing together, unless Aunt Izzie or Aunt Nuna or some other grown-up came along, too," she said.

Whatever the cause, Fanny Curtis did not marry Mr. Warner. Did she ever regret this? It is more likely that she briskly put marriage out of her mind that spring of 1899; she would have considered it a waste of time to keep looking backwards. She plunged more deeply into charitable and civic affairs. She had already served as a delegate to the National Conference on Charities and Corrections in 1898, in New York. While her stay here included the usual socializing, museum-going and shopping, these activities were merely peripheral to the real purpose of the trip. Days were filled with speeches, meetings and tours of tenement buildings. She wrote home: "This day began at nine with a visit, 200 strong, to the Mills Hotel—altogether too attractive a place for 1550 men who undoubtedly desert their tenemented families to live there at 20 cents a day...Just imagine—Aunt Annette went slumming till 2 o-clock Saturday night! She said that down in the Bowery, the Chinese quarter where she went, the streets were filled with people and they showed out at every window....Our organization of Charity Meetings here have been most exciting and crowded."

In 1899, Governor Wolcott appointed Frances G. Gurtis to the State Board of Charity. This position she held for fifteen years, as she was reappointed by succeeding governors. During this time she served on numerous committees. One of the most important was the Committee on the Inspection of Almshouses. The Legislature had just passed a bill requiring modernization of almshouses throughout the Commonwealth. These ranged from big institutions such as the one at Tewksbury to isolated and ramshackle farmhouses forlornly scattered throughout the state. All of them showed their common ancestry in the medieval "hospital" which contained any and all human beings who were discarded by society: paupers and cripples, old people, the mentally deranged, drunkards, orphans and criminals. Although there had been one or two attempts to improve almshouse conditions during the 19th century, this new legislation, requiring rigorous supervision on a regular schedule, brought about considerable change. Fanny Curtis took active and creative part in the Inspection Committee's work. As it was the duty of the committee to report annually the conditions in almshouses to the General Court, as well as draw up recommendations and speak before the Legislature, she became experienced in both, and her influence and interest in legislative matters soon extended into other areas of concern as well. Her work on the Inspection Committee, however, continued to take much of her time and effort. Although she had organized a task force of volunteer visitors, she did much of the inspecting of almshouses herself, and kept detailed account of each, regarding the welfare of inmates, plumbing and other repairs needed, a balance sheet and proposed budget. The work of the Almshouse Inspection Committee increased as the number of institutions increased during the early years of the 1900s. Between twelve and twenty almshouses were inspected monthly, and Fanny Curtis continued to do much of the visiting herself. As late as 1912, we find her writing to her sister Peg (away in London): "I have done Wrentham, Walpole, Canton, Tewksbury, Upton, Weston, Sherborn, Westfield—and yesterday Warren, en route to Lenox."

Perhaps Peggy understood the political currents swirling through the rest of the letter:

> ...I say there's nothing doing, but really the devil's in it at the State House—Governor Foss thinks now he can't get Pettigrove out—he can't get through the new defective cottages and Sherborn. Mr. Hodden is in despair, et., etc...continuous performance in the way of State Conference meetings—Prison Commissioner—feebleminded committee, etc...very perplexing State Board re. arrangements. My, there's so much news you can hardly see it. And speaking of new things, if you see a hat at my friend Miss Hobbes, Clifford Street, with this shade of blue—or black or burnt straw, purchase it for me.

With unfailing energy, Aunt Fan had really got into her full swing by 1904. A glance at her engagement calendar for March of that year shows no blank space amid its thirty-one days, and most of these are filled with three or four appointments: "Char Ass'n"—"State Ho"—"Civil Serv."—"Village Improvement"—"AlmsHo Comm"—"Dorchester Ct."—"Exec Comm St. Conf.". Interspersed with these commitments are lunches, teas and dinner parties, skating and bowling, concerts and opera, for Aunt Fan's boundless civic zeal was matched by her capacity for enjoyment. Her optimism and good health were apparently inexhaustible; she continued to give herself a full life decade after decade. Even in her late eighties she dashed out to an evening concert in Cambridge, taking the subway to Harvard Square because no Curtis sister ever wasted money on a taxi. Returning by subway, she emerged from the Park Street Station into a raging blizzard. She did remark the next day, however, that perhaps it was a trifle silly for someone at her age to be floundering through snowdrifts on Boston Common alone at midnight.

But let us return to her earlier activities. In 1903, Frances G. Curtis was sent as delegate to the National Conference of Charities and Corrections in Atlanta, Georgia. Following Curtis family custom, she wrote home four times during the week she was away, beginning with a postcard, "I believe I never mentioned that I expect to be at the Hotel Aragon, where you may write to me frequently." During the week, she wrote more fully:

> The conference is a great success, and is more full of business than an egg of meat....I had forgotten what a joy it is to come to one of these things and see and hear all these most interesting people—they certainly *are* interesting. And it is a great experience. Now I must go and tackle Jane Addams to get her to come to Boston next November for our conference.

Over the following years, Fanny was frequently called upon to represent her city and state at a variety of national conventions. As well as the Atlanta conference on charities, she attended a meeting in Richmond that same year, where the new and revolutionary concept of school playgrounds as a city responsibility was introduced. "The conference began last night *very* successfully," she wrote home. "Yesterday aft. I went to my reception at a Mrs. Reynolds's, and have seldom seen pandemonium like it. Truly, three rooms full of shrieking Richmond women can make *noise* enough to deafen the stranger."

In 1905 she was asked to give a paper at the national conference of social workers in Portland, Oregon. Ever ready to combine business with pleasure, she stopped at Yosemite Park on the way and wrote home ecstatically:

> I tell you it was a fine feeling last night, to look up through the boughs of my giant pine to where the Dipper was bending into the Falls as they came over the cliff just half a mile over my head. And the planets came twinkling up over the rim, too. We got up at 5, before the sun came up, so as to see the reflections in Mirror Lake. One of those fool expeditions that you can't help making ....I am simply wild over the flowers, imagine fields of lobelia both light and dark, and a fascinating little blue lily, and wild bouvardia of a salmon pink and white. And the banks of the Merced River are solid masses of white azalea with yellow splashes.

A few days later, having reached the West Coast, she wrote:

> I got hold of old John Muir in San Fran, thinking him a good guide to the region—but lor, he's so rhapsodicized he spins you from Flat Head Reservation in Oregon to the Hetch Hetchy Valley, equally inaccessible, and tells you all the things you

aren't seeing. I am still toiling with my miserable paper for Portland, and I think I am now ready to write it off, which is something—but bad enough it will be.

The conference in Portland was perhaps one of the few occasions when Fanny felt inadequate. Full of humility toward herself, she was full of admiration toward others:

> The Committee finished its labors this afternoon, and my remarks took just about ten minutes this morning, for Miss Lathrop thought I had better merely give the Mass. facts I know (not Mass *of* facts!) instead of my flowery paper. I fear she despises me for the poorness of it, but what matters it—she writes the best report that has yet been given, presides better than any of the Star men here, and is altogether one of the most humorous, delightful and wise people I've ever had the luck to be thrown with. She is one of the original Hull House Residents, is the master of the Insane question, was on the Ill. State Board, and yet looks just my own age. I must say that between her and Mr. Devine, who is four months younger than I, I feel a feeble-minded youth, with no mental development whatsoever.

But three years later, it was Fanny who was presiding, and apparently perfectly equal to her task. The National Conference of Charities and Corrections was held in Richmond in 1908, and many hundreds of delegates were there, representing forty states, the Massachusetts group alone numbering forty-three. The Conference held several sessions on the subject of Juvenile Courts. While a number of cities already had well-established courts separating young law-breakers from seasoned criminals, this judicial system was not yet widely used throughout the country. Frances G. Curtis presided over the sessions of the agenda devoted to Juvenile Courts. She obviously enjoyed her role, though the Conference's full program was long and rigorous, day after day. It was 1 o'clock in the morning when she wrote this letter to her mother:

> Dearest Madam,
> This is the first instant I have had in my room today, since leaving it at 9:10 this morning, a trifle late for the first meeting. It's a strenuous life certainly, and I thrive on it.

The job is practically over with only one more meeting for me to preside over—the more I do it, the better I like it. And its *so* much easier than speaking! We are going to be in the thick of starting a Juvenile Court Committee here and a difficult to manage meeting for it comes tomorrow afternoon....My latest love and firmest backer is Miss Martha Berry of Rome, Georgia, who has just left some lovely roses for me. I've already had roses, orchids, peonies, a cottonwool Christmas tree, and a choice selection of flowers from Brook Hill. I'm a popular personage.

Richmond friends of the family, too, wrote rave reviews of "Fan's Triumph:"

Sunday night St. Paul's Church was packed and Fan presided at what was conceded to be the great meeting of the conference. Fan on the platform in our most conservative church, reading from the lectern and taking precedence of all others was flanked on both sides by the leading clergymen and most distinguished citizens of all creeds, and called to her subject and its discussion the very cream of the crop....

Another friend of the Curtises was equally glowing in praise:

As for Fannie, she carried all before her. We were so excited during the days of the conference that we failed to keep the papers and could not get them when we tried, so some of the choice bits were lost—one especially we liked, a line which mentioned three women of national reputation—Miss Addams, Miss Richmond, Miss Curtis...but aside from the papers, everybody who saw her preside with wonderful tact, grace and dignity. She pleased all, for she managed to make the interesting ones speak and shut off the bores.

For a dozen years while Fanny was on the State Board of Charities, she was a delegate at conventions here and there across the country, speaking at or chairing meetings. She was in Buffalo, in Pittsburgh, in Atlanta, and she shared a platform with Booker T. Washington at Hampton Institute. She also sought out George Washington Carver, at Tuskegee, and visited the George Junior Republic with its founder, the famous prison reformer Thomas Mott Osborne.

And she never slackened her pace while at home in Boston. A

letter from her sister Hatty to Bella gives an idea of Fan's activity in 1907:

> Fan has a gang in t'other room of Dr. Putnam's—Mrs. Evans and Co—getting after Arthur & his Civil Service group. She had her Sewing Circle here today—a gang of the plainest women I ever saw. They eat hearty but didnt begin to get through the vol-au-vent & lobster salad....

Writing again to Bella, a week or so later, Hat reports:

> F.G.C. had 60 Almshouse visitors to lunch yesterday, and also a meeting of the Neighborhood Club hearing a nurse in charge of 1000 children tell of her work. Today she's off to Arlington to interview a possible school superintendant—having spent the morning working for Miss Clarke's Destitute Mothers....

These were the daytime activities only. Almost every evening, she was dining out, or having a dinner party at home—except in the Opera season; one year she attended every opera that was performed during April, except for two which she had to miss because of previously accepted dinner parties: Aida—Lohengrin—I Barbieri—Parsifal—Lucia—Walkure—Boheme—Rigoletto—Pagliacci. Oh well, what did it matter missing Carmen and Meistersinger? She'd seen Carmen enough times, anyway.

In the summer, when committee meetings had subsided, Fanny could throw her energy into a wide variety of activities for pure pleasure. At Manchester there was always tennis to play, and swimming, and a game called "Swimble," invented by the Curtises and played in front of the stable.[2]

Often there were visitors staying at Sharksmouth, and if these were not familiar with "The North Shore," Fan would take them driving in the open carriage or the dog-cart to see her favorite scenic spots. If there was a lunch-party in Ipswich, a little too far away to use the carriage, it was a simple matter to take the train to Prides Crossing and thence a cross-country

---

[2] It was a little like squash, in that you hit a ball with a racquet up against the huge slanting roof of the stable. The skill lay in calculating how and where it would carom off—hopefully not where your opponents expected it.

trolley car to Ipswich. If there was a good breeze for sailing, there was the "Dream," the Curtis's big sloop, lying at anchor, a seaman always aboard, ready to glide out of Kettle Cove into the open sea. However, every summer Fanny abandoned the charms of Manchester and home to make good long visits with friends in New Hampshire, the Adirondacks and Maine, where she annually went cruising with the Reynoldses.

And there was Europe, ever beckoning. After her trip with Bella in 1896, Fan was abroad again in '98, escorting her younger sister Peggy. In 1902, she took Lutie Pleasants with her, to France and Spain. But the trip in 1906 was absolutely thrilling, for it was in an AUTOMOBILE! Yes, actually touring through Italy and France in an automobile.

A Mr. Coolidge, though old, was adventurous. Fanny Curtis and Grace Payson gladly accepted his invitation to be his companions for this novel way of touring Europe. All three sailed together on the *S.S. Canopic*, arriving in Naples on March 11th.

Gd Hotel du Vesuve, Naples

...It would be hard to match what is doing with us-uns. We landed this morning at nine....We are on the water, with the old Castel del'Ovo just in front, and we have a beautiful suite of sunny rooms, with bathroom included.

The chauffeur has been waiting here since the first and so as all was ready we gave the machine a trial spin this afternoon out to Posilippo Baiae, Lake Averuns, Cumae, and in fact all the shore there is to the West—perfect heavenly weather, fairly good roads, a good automobile although not as large as a Pierce, and no racks for luggage—but everything simply perfect. It was enough to show that there really is no other way of travelling. We ran over *nothing* although we went very fast. And our boy is very nice and careful about hens and puppies of which the roads are full. Tomorrow at eleven we start for Sorrento or Amalfi— we don't know or care which. There's nothing like it—we just laughed for joy like all the country people we passed who look upon a bubble as a great joke *and* delight, and wave their hands and grin and do *not* say one word of backsheesh or soldi. Isn't that a triumph? But these roads are dusty. We wore our rubber coats and found them excellent for warmth and cleanliness....

60

She was still ecstatic the next morning, dashing off a few words before starting on the day's venture:

March 12th

My dearest Madam,

As I wrote last night, the sensations of flying through all the wonderful places of the world in one afternoon are indescribable. And as for seeing the country & the people, there is nothing like it.

Here we are off—I'll tell you more later.

We started at about 12 with ideas of Sorrento for lunch and Amalfi for the night—but lo and behold, a Bur-r-rst tire at Torso del Greco at half past 12 so we picked up a very good lunch, while the chauffeur mended the tire. Unluckily, it came on to rain so that from Castelmare here we had no view. The rain was not good for the hat, but otherwise it did no harm....

The adventurous trio spent a few delightful days in Rome, which was already full of Cabots, Longfellows and other Bostonians. But the car, after its efforts tripping from Naples to Rome, needed a good overhauling.

March 23rd

Dearest Madam,

We are sitting around this morning for what we finally hope is the last delay we are going to have. It *is* maddening to get ready to start 3 separate times. Oh dear me. All our valises ready to be covered with the enamel cloth & strapped on behind, and we all with our veils and hoods and ready these three hours!

All through the hill towns of Italy, through Switzerland and France, through breakdowns, cracked cylinders and flat tires, through hailstorms and rain, Fanny never ceased to praise the miracle of automobile travel. From the Grand Palace Hotel in Perugia she wrote:

I can tell you volumes, once I get started, of the views that glide by us as we climb hills and coast down them, and the way in which we found old Father Tiber sporting as a mere lad, up by Gubbio, in pale green, trimmed with white over the rocks! I was so glad to see that he wasn't always as dirt-colored as he is in Rome. The hills are very wintry-looking where the snow lies on them, but on their slopes the grass is very green, and in sheltered places the daffodils and baby's breath are out, while the olives really give their color to all the landscape.

We missed our homeward road yesterday afternoon—nearly the death of Granpa! [Mr. Coolidge] and I came back to Perugia over hills instead of by the river. In consequence, we had the most exciting climb into the city through a perpendicular gate as you might say, having climbed to it, as to Heaven, by a ladder so we seemed to be falling over backwards....[T]he little people at the Gate were so excited they waved us through without making us halt as otherwise is invariable. Later in the day, they told Lucien they didn't think the machine existed that could fly up *that* street.

Day after day, Fan's letters home traced her travels, through mountains and gorges, through banks of flowers in Southern France, and hordes of cattle at a fair in the Midi.

Running a car through successive groups of men and beasts is naturally slow work—in fact Lucien prefers to stop entirely. But when we come to a ten mile strip of perfectly straight and level road he *does* let her hum—and says we go to 72 kilos, which is 45 miles & jolly good fun it is too....

It must be a very healthful life to be in the open air all the day long like this. The only regret is not having the family along, too....

And to think that tomorrow is the last day of this joy....I wonder how I can bear to take a train, which goes not at the hour I name, but when itself chooses. No, this spoils one for ordinary travel.

There were many summers, of course, when Aunt Fan did not go to Europe, but stayed at home, in Manchester, making the most of every day. When she was not busy running the huge household, she was berrypicking or playing games, or off with Mr. Hooper in the farm-wagon digging up laurel bushes in the Magnolia woods to transplant at Sharksmouth. She also kept her managerial hand in by organizing the Kettle Cove Book Club, wherein the latest books were circulated among the shore residents. A member had two books to read each week, before these were passed on to the next member. Also, her enthusiasm for Hampton Institute had remained unabated ever since she visited it in 1902. In this interest her sister Hatty joined her, and together they raised funds summer after summer for this outstanding training school and college for Negroes in Virginia. What better place to find money than among the well-heeled summer residents of the fashionable North Shore? Each season they would arrange an afternoon party at somebody's grand estate, invite the whole North Shore, have a distinguished speaker and a concert by the Hampton Quartet. These were four black men of Hampton with magnificent voices, who sang spirituals in beautiful harmony and moving rhythm. The Quartet and the President of Hampton usually stayed at Sharksmouth for the weekend of the meeting.

In 1911, Aunt Fan made a splendid arrangement. "I boldly telephoned five minutes since to Jeffie," she wrote Hatty (who was off in New Hampshire for the moment). "He says '*Sure* — delighted to help a good thing. Glad to have the meeting on our portico."—and didn't so much as consult Clara for an instant! I think that the house of T. Jefferson Coolidge will really be good bait." Since T. Jefferson Coolidge, a direct descendant of Thomas Jefferson, had modelled his house on Jefferson's *Monticello*, indeed it was a good idea of Fan's—and particularly so as this second Monticello had a spectacular setting on the pinefringed headland at the seaward tip of Coolidge Point, and in its ample hall were a number of portraits by Gilbert Stuart.

Governor Mann of Virginia gave the main speech at this Hampton meeting, and President William Howard Taft presided. Ever the opportunist, Fan had suddenly realized he was nearby, vacationing at Prides Crossing only a few miles away. Of course he agreed to assist Hampton when she asked him, for he was a Trustee of the Institute as well as President of the United States.

Aunt Fan certainly was an opportunist, and very frequently a successful one, though not in a derogatory sense. Combined with her habitual optimism and general affection for her fellow beings, opportunism meant seizing the moment and turning it to advantage for everybody. As the oldest in the family, she had no need for more power; as the grand-daughter of a millionaire she had no need for money. She seemed to thoroughly enjoy putting her health and energy into bettering the community around her, be it within her own household or on a world scale. Aunt Fan tackled a problem facing a welfare committee meeting in rather the same way she tackled a game of tennis. It's fun to win—but it's a good game and fun to play, anyway. A frequent phrase of hers was "seize the moment," whether the moment was used to wash a couple of windows before an appointment, put in a persuasive telephone call to a committee member, or spring from the lunch table because the ice on the Sudbury River was perfect for skating this afternoon but might not be so tomorrow. Or, at a society bazaar, she would see just the right (or nearly right) teapot as a wedding present for Susie—thus killing three birds with one stone, as she needed to help the pathetically inept saleslady *and* the bazaar, anyway.

She was always on the lookout for happy coincidences and exchanges, for well she knew that one man's discard is another man's treasure. Thus it was not surprising to see a row of old jam jars between the Greek columns of the portico at 28 Mt. Vernon Street's front door one day. She had put them there because it was silly to throw them in the trash barrel when there are plenty of people *needing* glass jars, and one of these was sure to come along. Aunt Fan usually used half-sheets or the backside of old wedding invitations when writing to family members, but there is one on elegantly engraved stationery of the Essex County Club: "Well, Hat," she writes, "here 'tis Sunday morning, and I have just stopped in to pick up some bones, knowing that those Saturday Men's Doubles usually stay on for a good feed after their game, and there must be a T-bone or two lying around for our old man 'Aigy.'" ('Aigy was the aunts' Old English Sheepdog, named for Field Marshal Haig.)

There was a time, however, when Aunt Fan seized an opportunity which didn't actually exist. It was the autumn of 1953 or '54, and the Boston Symphony Orchestra had already begun its regular season of concerts, when she heard that poor Lizzie B. had broken her hip and would be laid up for months. Taking the subway, Aunt Fan arrived at Symphony Hall just as the regular

Friday afternoon concert-goers were filing into the auditorium. "Mrs. B.'s seat," she simply said to the doorman and passed through with the rest. She enjoyed many Friday afternoon concerts that season, but when she happened to meet up with her benefactor in the spring, Lizzie told her she had never subscribed for a symphony season ticket that year, at all. They both thought it a great joke.

In 1913, Frances G. Curtis was elected to the Boston School Committee. She was the first woman ever to serve on this Committee, and remained its only woman member for the next twelve years. Her election was mainly due to the influence of Joseph Lee, already an active Committee member of several years standing. He and Fanny had been good friends for years, sharing many interests. Aside from their mutual pleasure in river skating and charade parties, they had worked together often and vigorously in a variety of organizations devoted to civic improvements.

The time was ripe for a woman on the School Committee. The year before Fanny was elected, the proposition of a woman member had become a lively issue in the election campaign. The S.V.A., a large organization of school-teachers, wanted a woman on the board to truly represent their interests. The Mayor wanted to enlarge the School Committee from five to nine members, in the hope of breaking up Joe Lee's "Clique" and thought he could get the School teachers' backing if he promoted a woman committee member. The "Clique" was supported by P.S.A., the Public School Association, whose membership included many Old Boston family Protestant Yankees, whereas the Mayor's backers were mainly New Boston Catholic Irish. At that time the rift between the two factions was wide. However, there was a woman candidate running for the School Committee, that year of 1912, a Mrs. Fitzgerald. She was the mother of nine children currently in the Boston school system, but she was not elected, although she got a very respectable number of votes. So Joseph Lee, astutely aware of the public's interest, promoted Frances G. Curtis as a candidate the following year, for the School Committee.

She campaigned vigorously. Shortly before election day, she

was approached by a *Boston Herald* reporter who asked her how she was standing the long campaign. Miss Curtis replied with a smile, "You behold before you a candidate who does not know fatigue." Persisted the reporter,"But don't you feel the strain of speaking every night?" to which she declared, "I was never sick in my life, and I never felt better than I do now." The report continued: "and indeed, with her radiant color and brilliant smile, erect carriage and vivacious manner, Miss Curtis was the picture of health, repose and good spirits."

The *Boston Herald* further reported that Miss Curtis had been for thirteen years a member of the State Board of Charity, and for the past six years she had been chairman of the subcommittee on the State's Minor Wards with 4,700 children under her care. She had been a director of the Massachusetts Civic League, chairman of the National Playground Association, vice president of the Drama League of Boston and a member of the Bowdoin School Neighborhood Association. She had been secretary of the Boston Cooperative Building Association and was director of Improved Dwellings for several years.

Once elected, she soon was recognized as a major force on the School Committee. Like Joseph Lee, she was involved in countless tasks and committee work arranging for space, equipment and supervision of playgrounds, as well as the regular on-going duties of building maintenance, teaching staff and salary problems. Frequently both confidante and ally of Joseph Lee, she came to be regarded as his other half. It was often her vote that carried the weight of board decisions in his favor. Ultimately, she wielded as much power as he did. "If you should happen to meet Joseph Lee or Miss Curtis," began a letter from John Kelly to Dr. Warren, "it might be worthwhile to help out the possible sale to the city.... I think they will be in the market in the next few years for a new Boston Latin School." Joseph Lee *or* Miss Curtis: both were regarded as the major components of the Committee for several years, until Joe Lee was not re-elected in 1917. The loss of Lee from the Committee did not appear to diminish Fanny's strong standing in the Committee, however, nor prevent the public from voting for her on her own merit. She continued to work zealously for the next seven years. A letter from her to her sister Bella (in Italy at the time) gives a good idea of how her days were spent:

> Dear Bol. Busy? Well rather! and what is more, busy in every department and all along the line. This week is a sample. Monday. A morning inspection of 3 South Boston schools in Ellen's motor after a hairwash & wave. Lunch Club at Mrs. Tyson's —a most tiresome affair with Elise Wadsworth laying down the law on the Social Evil till I nearly spat. Then a delightful hour at Discussion Club on "The best Equipment for Middle Age"—Mrs. Hig, Helen, Alice Ropes and so forth. Then at 4 to School Committee hearings, legislative matters & straight business, till home at 11. (I had to refuse opera and dinner & Copey at Rose Forbes.)

On and on her letter goes, describing each day's activities during the week. These averaged *eight* separate engagements per day, ranging from lecturing in Dorchester on child welfare to delighting in wire-haired terriers at the Dog Show; from a conference with school truant officers to dining out at the Alec Sedgwicks. How *could* she keep up this pace?

Unlike Joseph Lee, Aunt Fan was an early proponent of the Equal Work/Equal Pay demands of the female teachers; though not a teacher herself, she was sympathetic to their demands. She maintained a close relationship between the Board and the individual schools and staff. When Joe Lee drafted her bid for reelection in 1916, he included the following:

> Miss Curtis has been impersonal in her consideration of school problems, has invariably supported the progressive policy and the rule of the expert....She has also shown a more unusual quality—the power to say No, a quality essential to the useful-ness of any member of a School Committee....

Though kept busy with Committee work year after year, Fanny was also involved in many other causes. As World War I gradually overtook America's originally aloof attitude, the Curtis sisters became more involved. They opened the Boston house for a bazaar and attended many speeches by visiting leaders of France and England. Fan arranged a meeting for the poet John

Masefield to plead support for British hospitals caring for the wounded. Meanwhile, she continued her strenuous rounds of School Committee duties and became more deeply enmeshed in plans for the establishment of a Women's City Club. "Francie is busy as ever," wrote her mother, "though she catches time to go to lunch club today in Chestnut Hill, and play bridge anywhere, anytime—trimming the little nieces' hats between whiles."

In 1925, Frances G. Curtis decided to resign from the School Committee and run for Mayor of Boston. A fellow School Committee member, David Scannell, also planned to leave the board and wrote her the following pencilled note at their last meeting:

> As I have said more times than I recall, you have been 1 woman in 1,000,000 in your ready and fine adjustment to a Board almost entirely masculine: it has been as easy to talk things over with you and debate them as with any man. Differences of opinion (which have been wonderfully few) have never left rancor. You have been a wonderful associate, and I am glad to go off with you.

But running for Mayor of Boston in 1925 was no simple matter. That year, instead of the usual two or three candidates seeking the office, there were over a dozen. Fan called Joe Lee for help, but by this time Joe had receded from city politics, and also expressed reservations about supporting a woman for mayor:

> I know that you have a great and deserved popularity with all branches throughout the city. I guess you could get a majority among the Catholics for School Committee, but I don't think these same people want a woman mayor. I don't feel I ought to go in, even to the extent of an endorsement....

Fan went ahead anyway. Under the headline, "MAYORAL SITUATION HAS POLITICIANS RUNNING RAGGED," the *Boston Evening Transcript* wrote the following:

> With thirteen alleged bona fide candidates already entered in the race and utter confusion prevailing, the situation has taken a new turn within 24 hours. In the announcement of Miss Frances Curtis of the School Committee that she is a candidate for

mayor, the first woman in the City's history seeks election as its chief executive.

Miss Curtis has issued a business-like announcement which, like all political documents of its kind should be, definitely assumes she will win, for it states: "My appeal should be directly to the voters, men and women, as my responsibility shall be to them, only, when I am elected."

Joe Lee's predictions proved true, however, and by October Frances G. Curtis was out of the running. Nevertheless, it is significant that she had the initial support as well as her own gumption to throw her cap into the ring. That in itself was an astonishing act in 1925.

Aunt Fan took her defeat in stride; there were plenty of other things that needed doing, and which indeed could be accomplished better outside of public office. To these she turned with undampened spirit. One of her greatest interests was the League of Nations, and the need to strengthen support for it among Americans. Despite the betrayal of Woodrow Wilson's greatest hope for strong and useful membership of the United States in this world organization, the League of Nations was extremely active all through the 1920s and was the prime instrument for settling international disputes and maintaining world peace. Aunt Fan naturally wanted to learn about it at its source and had visited Geneva for several weeks in September 1923, before her School Committee duties began. In characteristic manner, she quickly made her way into the inner circles of officialdom:

> *September 3, 1923*
> *Hotel Regina, Geneva*
>
> Well, dear fellers, its more exciting than you'd suppose when I say that actually this morning all that was done in the hour and a half of the meeting was a series of resolutions on the Japanese earthquake, and this afternoon we only elected the new President which was done by voting as the names of countries were called and without any nominations nor nothing: while Cuba was welcomed to his place in the chair by Japan, he pulled his speech of acceptance out of his pocket at once. However, the actual fact of all those 52 sitting there side by side is the Real Thrill.

Manley O [Hudson] is right up to the mark: he had a ticket for all the sessions ready with my name on it this morning...and then he invited me to lunch to meet Fridtjof Nansen and Dame Rachel Crowdy and 15 others at the International Club. And between him and Lady Ames we have got almost all the gossip going on Mussolini and various attitudes thereto....Needless to say the Council is meeting like mad to discuss Italy. Nansen is absolutely sure it will come out right—if not, and Mussolini really flouts the L. of N., the whole Scandinavian section will resign and break up the League!...The impression among all the Americans and English was that France was doing all she could to back Mussolini in order to get the same freedom in the Ruhr, but was somewhat restrained by fears of what the little Entente would say....[Y]ou feel you can hardly bear to wait till the morning....

Geneva, Sept. 8th

I am just back from the luncheon party at the Ames's, where I sat on Lord Robert Cecil's right and had the very merriest ha ha for an hour and a half that I could ask for, and when we did pause, I could fire a few questions at Mr. Hood, Minister for Education. It *was* good, and I told Lady Ames what I thought of her, after. Incidentally, I passed the time of day with Count Mensdorf and he told me I need have no fear of any difficulty in getting to and fro Vienna....

I am writing this while waiting for the Committee to gather and hear Zimmerman give an account of the restoration of Austria. The Maharajah Singh is presiding and we are guessing the nationalities of all the men down the long tables...I feel now that the only man I have yet to see is the Sec. Gen. Sir Eric Drummond, and of course Lady Ames will see to that. Meanwhile we tremble and tremble and wonder if Lord Robert will pull the thing off. Sir Herbert says that it seems hard to believe that the whole thing is in his hands and that he is pushing and pushing little by little until soon he will have them—France and incidentally Italy, in the place where he can tie things up.

...Lemme see, have I written since the cruel scene of M. Hudsons's lunch for Lord Robert when he insisted on my coming—and I had got Dame Rachel already, so that I simply couldn't go? But Lord Robert's remarks were brought over to us instantly, to the effect that he felt on the whole content with the process of negotiations. The question is, How will the lack of dramatic action please the American public? Are they going to say that this proves its uselessness, or will they say that if it had not been for the League Greece would have been wiped out long since,—which is what Lord Robert says, proving that if only as the place Greece could appeal to, the League had justified its existence....

Twas perfectly amazing, the number of Americans in that gallery this morning. We knew a good many, like Miss Dudley and the Bazeley family, and Charles Eliot & other youths from Harvard...but twas a pleasure to look down on Paderewski and wife in lower balcony, and watch him play five-finger exercises on the rail, while talking. He was in the Distinguished Visitors' Gallery.

Before sailing for home that September, Aunt Fan dashed off to Vienna and Poland and then to her favorite city, London. Here she had a chance to hobnob with her friend Sir Horace Plunkett before going to Oxford, because the poet John Masefield had written her a cordial note inviting her out to Boar's Hill (just outside Oxford) for an evening.

On returning to Boston, she went to work publicizing the vital importance of the League and building the League of Nations Association into a strong organization with widespread membership. The headquarters of the Assocation was established at 40 Mt. Vernon Street—just three doors down the street from the Curtis house, so it was a simple matter for Aunt Fan to be in almost daily consultation with Miss Irene Armstrong, the Association's executive secretary. Together they planned meetings and arranged speaking engagements for distinguished authorities on international affairs.

But international understanding was not the only interest of Aunt Fan's during the twenties. Her years of working in the public domain had made her an increasingly positive individual, whose independent ideas were heeded by women and men alike. She never fussed about "male domination" or women needing to break out of their traditional shackles. If someone was doing a good job, it didn't matter if that person was male or female.

*"This is incredible...,"
she writes of this 1932
Nazi pamphlet*

*"Keep,"
she writes
in October
of 1911*

Aunt Fan was always responsive to current happenings.

She never was an active suffragette, though it was obvious she believed in equal citizenship as early as 1911, when she wrote "KEEP" at the top of a women's suffrage pamphlet.

The Women's City Club took up much of Aunt Fan's time and energy in the twenties. The club had been started in 1913 by a Miss Bruorton, who wanted to establish a large democratic club for women, similar to the Men's City Club. She enlisted Helen Storrow and Frances G. Curtis to organize it. The Club's objectives were "to promote a broad acquaintance among women; to maintain an open forum where leaders in matters of public import and civic interest may be heard frequently; and to provide a clubhouse where its members may meet informally." Aunt Fan and Helen Storrow set to with a will. They recruited members, set up meetings with interesting speakers, hiring halls or hotel space for these, while all the time searching for the perfect headquarters. After a few years, the club was able to buy 40 Beacon Street, a beautiful and commodious mansion opposite Boston Common, which for the next seven decades would be the home of the Women's City Club. Aunt Fan and Helen Storrow were great friends, and saw eye to eye on many subjects, both civic and sporting, work and play. Helen Storrow was the Club's first president, and Aunt Fan several times thereafter.

Her zeal to see the Club thrive with an evergrowing membership and a rich program of events, lectures and entertainments kept her well occupied—but not to the exclusion of other matters. The League of Nations Association needed constant enhancing (and there was a chance that the Albanian Embassy might move to Boston), and a plan to build a new hospital to care for Boston's growing Negro population required many conferences at 28 Mt. Vernon St. attended by medical and civic leaders. Ultimately, this proposition was abandoned. "The hospital is no go," Aunt Fan wrote to an absentee sister, and turned her attention elsewhere. She was on the Board of the "Survey," journal of the New York School of Social Work, and regularly attended its meetings in New York (usually travelling there by bus). She also travelled around Massachusetts, for she was much in demand as a speaker in the Women's Club circuit.

Meanwhile, she always had time for an evening's dinner party, opera, or game of bridge. In the daytime, between appointments, she would fit in a chapter or two of a detective story, or touch up a scarred bit of the parlor wainscotting with a few brush-strokes of white paint. Or, if Mrs. Kilgallen (a marvelously picturesque little toothless cleaning woman) failed to appear, Aunt Fan tackled the window-washing job herself.

Her global interests increased. She and Aunt Hat became interested in an agricultural school in Salonika, Greece. This was run by Dr. Charles House, the brother of the directress of a school for Negroes in South Carolina who was a dear friend of Aunt Bog (who, in turn, frequently visited Penn School on St. Helena Island). Aunts Fan and Hat raised funds among their Boston friends to supply modern equipment for the Salonika school, while Aunt Bog collected donations of money and clothing for Penn School in South Carolina.

But the Aunts did not only focus their energies on institutions. There were a number of individuals who, stranded at one time or another, had become friends and protegées, and were frequently members of the Curtis household for weeks or months at a time. There was Jennie Lawton, whom Aunt Pedge had found sitting on a bench in the Common, in tears because she had failed in her ambition to become a Boston policewoman, and had nothing to go back to in Athol, Massachusetts. She was a household member on and off for a number of years. The Aunts called her "Hiram," and found various occupations for her, and delighted in her up-country sense of humor. Jeanne Roulet of France was another protegée. I never knew what her hard luck had been, way back in the 1890s, but the Curtis sisters, including my mother, were all concerned with her temperamental ups and downs, her concert career and her marriage to a Monsieur Pavey. Each of the Curtis sisters in turn became her confidante, and, of course, they all compared notes with each other, following the usual Curtis custom of ignoring privacy. There are many letters still extant of Fan's, Bella's and Elly's, all about Jeanne, full of advice, annoyance and compassion.

Aunt Fan, in particular, had a number of "Lame Ducks," as

she called them, and the most outstanding of these was Lutie Pleasants. Lutie was an impoverished Southern gentlewoman from Richmond. When the Curtis sisters first met her at Satty Fairchild's tea party for her in 1897, she was wearing an enamelled Confederate flag pin on her lapel. She was somewhat deaf, had a cleft palate and a harelip. None of these got in the way of her keen enjoyment of life, her dauntless spirit and peals of laughter. Aunt Fan soon took her under her wing, and there she was for many years. Lutie came for long visits in Boston and Manchester. Aunt Fan arranged for her to learn the antique art of painting trays, so that she could earn real money from the sale of these exquisitely finished replicas, replete with sprays of old-fashioned flowers bordered with golden scroll-work. Aunt Fan then saw to it that her rich Bostonian friends bought Lutie's masterpieces to give as wedding presents.

She also took Lutie traveling. In 1902, when Bella Curtis was visiting the Pleasants family in Richmond, Fan wrote her that "Uncle Henry" (Higginson) had just given her $1000, and she had half a mind to blow it on taking Lutie to Europe. What did Bella think? Was Lutie strong enough to go? She certainly was; and they had a wonderful tour of Italy and Spain. In 1928, Aunt Fan took Lutie abroad again, this time to England. I was in London, too, that summer, and Aunt Fan roped me in to join them at the House of Lords to have tea on the terrace with Lady Astor. "Nanny Astor" was a friend of long standing with both Aunt Fan and Lutie, for as Nancy Langhorne, she had grown up in Virginia, and knew all the Pleasants tribe. She and Aunt Fan could both understand Lutie's speech. (I was continuously bewildered; she would emit vowel sounds but very few consonants.) While "Nannie" and Lutie were talking and were out of earshot, Aunt Fan told me with great satisfaction how she had saved "Lute" from catching pneumonia the day before.

They had gone by bus to Kew, to visit its beautiful gardens and palace. But when, on leaving, they stepped outside the palace door, it had started to rain—in fact, it was raining cats and dogs. The highway and bus stop were a good quarter-mile away, at the end of the long avenue leading to the palace. But what luck! An elegant private limousine stood before the palace door, its liveried chauffeur in place behind the wheel, awaiting his aristocratic employers. "So I quickly popped Lute into the front seat," said Aunt Fan, "and told the chauffeur to let her out at the end of the driveway, where I'd meet her. Ha! wasn't that a piece of luck!" "It certainly was," I congratulated her. Then, when she had turned back to chat with the others, I silently amused myself with picturing the owners of the limousine, on finding a strange lady in the front seat, questioning her politely, and being answered by a few barks of unfathomable syllables. How like Aunt Fan! I knew just how she carried it off, with that friendly but very decisive smile of hers to the chauffeur, as she pushed Lutie in beside him, and doubtless, when the limousine stopped at the end of the avenue to let Lutie out, she had some charming exclamation about "true friends in time of need," and a merry laugh, as she thanked the bewildered couple in the tonneau. Her bright comment and laugh would leave no room for retort or complaint on their part; in fact, as was customary in her encounters, she probably left them feeling pleased with themselves for their generous action.

Tea on the terrace of the House of Lords was only one of the delights Lady Astor provided for her old friends from America. A letter of Aunt Fan's to her family tells more:

> *Thursday, June 14, 1928*
> *On the river at Hampton Court*

And this is the tale of our London Season, not yet a week old. Our first day we celebrated at Olympia—methinks I gave you our emotions already—Then Sunday to hear Kreisler, a bitter disappointment, for not one note did Lute hear—Monday, cant seem to remember what red letters that represented, but Tuesday: Lunch with Lady Astor in St. James's Square—a nice neighbor couple from Cornwall—sister Phyllis Branch & 4 children beginning with "my son Bobby Shaw." Afterwards, they all traipsed off to a wedding,—but not before Nanny had said, however, "look here, why don't you girls come and see my dance tonight—its such fun to look on when you don't have any responsibilities"—we said it was, and thought no more but later in the afternoon her Sec. telephoned to say Lady Astor was counting on our coming without fail. As you may well believe, I couldn't have held Lute back if I had wanted to, and at eleven you may see us mounting the traditional London stairs—egged on by flunkies all the way up, and Nanny Astor greeting us "here are my girls, the *real* debutantes!", and leading us to a sofa that commanded the ballroom—and who in close attendance but Maurice Baring! most friendly, most reminiscent, most keen to talk about his books, and eager to make a date for tea in his own home (Dartmouth House). Hostess came up at short intervals with men till we told her to forget us. A nice one sat down suddenly beside me saying "I am Nanny's husband"—and the final touch was to have Jack Balfour appear, and almost throw his arms around my neck!

As we explained when Nanny led us in to supper, one on each arm, we had *never* known such a nice party—And it was so gay and simple that you couldn't imagine it to be London. The first people I recognized were Winston Churchill dancing with Lady Diana Cooper, while nice Mr. J. Ridgely Carter pointed out all the Abercorn descendants in the room!...The standard of looks and dresses was very high—but you can imagine my joy when I asked Mr. Carter the name of the very charming elder woman on a neighboring sofa and he answered "oh, you mean the Duchess of Devonshire"! And on our saying to Nanny on leaving that we were charmed to have seen her, she called out, "Mary, come here and meet my two Virginia buds"—and Mary came right over....

How Aunt Fan rejoiced in High Society—particularly English Nobility! It was not exactly snobbery; it was more like a game with her, probably originating with all those Victorian novels the Curtis girls read (with their mother's approval) wherein the modestly raised heroine is politely carried across a raging mountain torrent by a kindly young man who turns out to be an Earl. (Sometimes she is endangered by a shipwreck, or other difficulty, but the hero is always very well-born.) But basking in the glow of aristocracy was not Aunt Fan's chief occupation. Concerned about Lutie's plight in a rainstorm, she was equally concerned with the well-being of Mrs. Kilgallen, the cleaning woman, whom she regarded as a friend (and often quoted "Kilgal's" witticisms). In the great influenza epidemic of 1918, when there was a disastrous shortage of nurses, she had spent long hours tending little children in a hospital ward. And she was always dropping in on disabled friends of hers, cheering them with her optimistic outlook, as well as her sympathy.

Her smiling approach to circumstances was successful again and again during Aunt Fan's long and variegated public career. Back when she was a member of the Boston School Committee, I once listened to her swaying a recalcitrant fellow-member on the telephone. It was all done in a quiet voice, in a few words interspersed with chuckles. "Ha! So glad I could reach you! It's F.G. here ... Exactly, exactly!...(chuckle)...Well, *we* say it's only a matter of time before...Oh, of course!...(chuckle)...Yes, yes! Ha!...Well, *we* think if old man Kelly...yes, exactly! Isn't he... (chuckles) Yes, that's it. Ha!...So glad you agree," and she hangs up. Another vote on the right side.

During the nineteen-twenties, Aunt Fan became interested in the farm cooperatives then being developed in China. Mao Tse Tung, as a young man, had done much traveling in Central China where he had been shocked by the oppressive conditions under which the peasants were forced to live. Later, as a recognized leader, he organized a number of Peasant and Industrial Unions and in 1926 he established the Kuomintang's Peasant Training Institute, with himself as director. Aunt Fan took to the cause of Chinese Industrial Cooperatives with vigor. She learned all she could about the pitiful condition of the peasantry and the movement to remedy it. She carried on much correspondence with Rewi Alley and other backers of the Chinese cooperative movement and promoted the cause among her friends at home. Cooperatives at that time were successfully operating in Scandinavia, and in the thirties, Franklin Roosevelt was interested in their development as a remedy for American farmers ruined by Dust Bowl disasters.

With never-slackening pace, Aunt Fan pursued her wide variety of interests and even added to their roster. She and Aunt Hat took up lessons in pottery-making, turning out a number of vases and bowls, often with a beautiful greeny-blue glaze over a Persian design. After 1928, when Aunt Hat became Dean of Women at Hampton Institute in Virginia, Fan wrote to her frequently. These letters were often in pencil, written from the second balcony of Symphony Hall during intermission, or from Ford Hall Forum before the speaking began. The following was written after returning to Manchester from that splendid trip to England with Lutie Pleasants:

Manchester, October 14, '28

Hattay—I must send you this letter for I think it is a real tribute, as I have written Rose herself—and long may all these good points last—health—hygiene—cheerfulness—self confidence, interests in people, places art and letters!...I have been out for my Annual Game: I played nine holes with Peg this morning early— then some tennis with Mr. Appleton vs. the Young. And then walked around and about Dana Beach this heavenly p.m. with the Raymond family. So I feel well exercised. But I have never been more than warm—oh the difference from Friday night on the stage of Mechanics Hall in the biggest crowd you ever saw, to hear Gertrude Ely and Franklin Roosevelt when we all mopped and mopped in the heat. Of course in running for the 9:30 train, I just missed Franklin, and they all say he was marvelously moving. He has to walk with a man's arm, like K.S....

Friday eve, Oct. 19

...Thursday, I passed a hectic morning, because I was trying to get the lunch party together that Nannie Astor wanted—Fred Cabot, Felix Frankfurter, and Dr. Miriam Van Waters who is doing some special research work for Frankfurter. I finally got em all but Nannie was dreadfully late....She is just as charming and natural as in London....

October 19, 1930

Hattay. I am finding it absurdly difficult to place the Incas but am now on my way to the Athenaeum for knowledge—almost as hard as to write a chapter on "Woman's Sphere" in Boston in the last 50 years! I can place Mrs. Eddy and the Mother Church, Mrs. Gardner and Fenway Court, the Woman's Club movement, and the young in business, and after that I am nowhere.

Although Aunt Fan's interests were scattered locally and globally, and her energies pulsated somewhat erratically among them, two of them have become long-lasting Boston institutions. One, the Women's City Club, has been already cited. The other is the Boston Center for Adult Education. Aunt Fan was a founder of this, first working persistently to spread the concept of Adult Education and to raise money for its establishment; she then was successful in procuring a building for its operation (putting a good deal of her own money into its purchase). This is 5 Commonwealth Avenue, once the home of an affluent Boston family. Its generous proportions include a ballroom, now named "Frances Greely Curtis Hall." Founded in 1933, the Center now provides hundreds of people annually with a wealth of courses ranging from archaeology to modern languages and cooking. It has become so popular that an annex has been added on Arlington Street.

When the Center was first established, there were opening ceremonies in Curtis Hall, and of course Aunt Fan was there on the platform in the place of honor. She gave a short speech herself, but didn't wait to receive the ones in her praise because she wanted to catch the evening train home to Manchester. When she got home, the other aunts were still up. "Francey! You *didn't* wear those shoes sitting on the platform!" said one. "Was your petticoat showing all the time the way it is now?" asked another. Aunt Fan glanced down at her out-sized bargain-basement men's shoes, and said, "Oh well." She correctly recognized these sisterly greetings as signs of approval.

Serene and alert, Aunt Fan moved through decade after decade, always interested in the world around her, always physically active. She had given up skating by the time she was eighty, but still liked to play a game or two of tennis—provided her partner would do all the running. She also took many walks; when in Boston, she would go downtown several times a week on shopping errands, across the Common and into the busy throngs around Jordan Marsh and Filene's Basement. In Manchester, she set off almost every morning by winding path or roadway to drop in at one of the other houses on the place and chat with whoever of its occupants were at home. She enjoyed picking blackberries and blueberries. In the blackberry season, she walked off into the woods, armed with a basket, to her favorite patches, where she stood entangled waist-deep in briars, picking and picking until her basket was full.

In 1954, when the House UnAmerican Activities Committee was holding hearings in Washington and Senator McCarthy was at his most rampant, I dropped in at the Aunts' one summer morning. Aunt Fan was standing, feet apart in her characteristic pose, briskly beating the morning newspaper against her thigh. She was then eighty-seven years old and afire with indignation. "I wish he'd summon *me* down there, for I certainly have something to say to *him*!" "Why Aunt Fan, why should McCarthy want to summon you?" I asked. "Because of those Chinese Cooperatives! Ha!" she replied. But she never got a chance to tell him off to his face. Too bad, because she was raring to go and would have been very effective.

She was equally lively two years later, when she accosted me in July: "Ib, I'm going to give myself a treat for my Ninetieth birthday—'Antony and Cleopatra' will be playing in New York on January 23rd, and I propose you and I go and see it. How about it?" I said, "Sure!" "Then I'll order tickets right now and get the best seats in the house." She did. Six months later I joined her in the 2nd row, center, before the curtain went up. We had gone to New York separately, I to visit an old college friend, she a few days earlier, to stay with her friend Charles C. Burlingham, a grand old nonegenarian, known to many as the "First Citizen" of New York. "Aunt Fan! What wonderful seats!" I greeted her, "but too bad you didn't ask Charlie Burlingham to join you, instead of just me." "Not at all," she replied, "deaf as a post and blind as a bat." The performance was marvelous. But we did not stay to the end. Just as Cleopatra was applying the asp to her bosom, Aunt Fan arose, muttering "C'mon, my girl," and we climbed over many knees to our exit. The five o'clock train to Boston must not be lost—and here we were, way over on Seventh Avenue, uptown, blocks and blocks away from the Grand Central Station. Of course we didn't take a taxi, but scurried on foot, each carrying one of her paper bags (her only luggage) and arrived with ten minutes to spare. "I'll meet you at the foot of the steps," said she, making for the porter's luggage ramp, herself, because she "didn't like" stairs. When I got down the long flight she was there, and we still had time to find the right track, walk past several cars to one up front, right behind the dining car. I settled her in a seat near the door, saying "There now, this is good, because you won't have any trouble getting to the dining car." "Oh no, my dear! I never use a diner! I've got my dinner here," she said. Reaching into one of her paper bags, she pulled out a little packet wrapped in waxed paper. "I got Margaret to make me a turkey sandwich before I left Boston, and it's been sitting in Charlie Burlingham's refrigerator ever since. Ha! How's *that* for foresight!" She was smiling contentedly as I left her.

That summer of 1957, she began to slow down a bit. She was willing to start the day later by having her breakfast brought to her in bed. She still took her daily walk, but it was shorter—and why not? She was well over ninety, and her steps had become a trifle tottery. On the morning of August 19 she wrote a letter to her friend Mark Howe, telling of her renewed pleasure in reading Emerson's essays, and another to Miriam Van Waters, congratulating her for her great work in improving women prisoners' conditions. Then she was ready to go downstairs. But once started, she apparently decided to go back to her room and exchange her shoes for sneakers. They found her, sneaker in hand, fallen beside her bed.

Among old letters in her desk I later came across a typewritten slip of paper:

> The people on the shore stood watching as the ship sailed out to sea. Presently her hull, then sails and topmast sank out of sight, below the horizon. "There! she's gone," they said. But on the other side of the water, people stood watching. "Here she comes!" they said.

Aunt Bog, c. 1890

Chapter Five

Aunt Bog
Isabella Curtis 1872-1966

The next in age of our aunts after Aunt Fan was Isabella Curtis, called "Beast," "Bulky," "Isab," "Bolla" by her siblings and "Aunt Bog" by us nieces, probably because she gave in to us so easily when we asked for another piece of candy. She was a great favorite of ours, for she treated us as real people—not just children to teach how to do things. We were her companions on morning expeditions through the woods, and at tea-time, a daily ceremonious rite she practiced. After we had sipped our weakened Lapsang Souchong from scalloped Italian teacups, and after the tea tray had been removed, Aunt Bog often read aloud to us.

The morning expeditions, walking through the woods, were almost daily excursions to hunt down and destroy Gypsy Moth nests. These moths were a scourge, attacking and denuding much of Massachusetts forest lands in the early decades of the 20th century. Aunt Bog, dressed in a faded smock and the shabbiest of khaki skirts, and armed with a can of creosote, would lead off into the woods, followed by a procession of dogs and children. Our job was to scramble about among the trees, finding the moths' nests—fuzzy, cream-colored, oblong humps about the size of a quarter, stuck on bark, stumps and boulders by the prolific female Gypsies. "Here's one!" a niece would shout, and Aunt Bog would aim for the cry, carefully nursing her creosote can through the underbrush to where one of us stood pointing. With a house-painter's sash-brush she then coated the nest completely with the deadly creosote. Our grandmother would often join us for the hunt, and sometimes we finished off the morning with a little bonfire of brushwood. We sat around roasting apples, while Granny sat on a rock of appropriate height. What fun it was! We all enjoyed ourselves, while doing something important at the same time.

And it was always fun when Aunt Bog read aloud, after tea. There was a stack of books, some illustrated by Randolph Caldecott and others by Walter Crane, kept in a cupboard under the magazine table. We would huddle around Aunt Bog on the sofa while she brought to life each tale, slowly turning pages from one fascinating illustration to the next. She dramatized what she was reading so well that Cinderella's sisters were horrifying, the Frog Prince overwhelmingly handsome, and John Gilpin an extraordinarily important horseman. As for Orson and Valentine, I wonder about them to this day. Was the legend based on fact? Did King Pepin really have twin sons, one brought up as a prince, the other raised by a bear in the forest surrounding ancient Paris? Anyway, it was wonderful that King Pepin, out hunting one day, found the wild and shaggy Orson and brought him home to join his brother Valentine.

We loved Aunt Bog's dramatic sense; but with her sisters, also, she frequently dramatized, making extreme remarks and fierce criticisms. Why this hostility, when it was obvious she was devoted to them—and they to her? Through all their long lives together, her sisters were the daily targets of her witty sarcasms and sharp retorts. Why was this necessary to her? Did she begin as a child to crave attention? It would be only natural, since she was in the middle of that mass of Curtis children; the fifth-born of the ten, she may easily have felt overlooked between the four boisterous older ones and the five younger ones who needed so much of her mother's attention, after each was born. And much of her mother's care was spent on her hero-husband. Did Isabella start out by unconsciously copying her martial father, that outspoken martinet and, after the Civil War, a semi-invalid, to get attention? Were her verbal roundshots and life-long various maladies all unconscious means of arousing and holding loving concern? We have already seen, in a previous chapter, how easily she discarded her ailments to thoroughly enjoy

London high life with her sister Fan in 1896. But by then a mother-daughter link had been firmly welded in which Isabella was both victor and victim. She became debilitated with head-aches; she suffered from sleeplessness. She developed a "bad" knee and attacks of neuralgia. Her mother may have been the chief perpetuator of her illnesses, for she asked Bella every day how her head felt and how she had slept. If Bella was away visiting, an anxious postcard reached her daily, asking the same questions. Even when she was abroad, having a delightful trip through Italy with a friend, her mother wrote, "You and Liz seem to be enjoying yourselves thoroughly—but in your letters you make no mention of your head, or sleeping ability. It will be well if you keep a chart of the hours of sleep you are getting each night, and send the record to me."

It is obvious from her many sprightly letters that when away from home, Bella was not a sufferer. Visiting in New York as a twenty-year-old, she had a marvelous time, with handsome young men lining up to be introduced so they could dance with her. Four years later, she was in Santa Barbara for a good long visit and playing golf every day to improve her game. Often during her twenties and thirties, she was in South Berwick, Maine, with her friend Liz Tyson, whose family's beautiful old house beside the river was the scene of numerous house parties. These always included a suitable number of eligible bachelors to match the three or four of her favorite girlfriends that Liz had invited. Bella was often the witty and charming center of a merry evening beside the fire, after an active day of sports, picnicking and canoeing, or in the winter of skating, snow-shoeing, tobogganing and sleigh rides.

But when Bella was living at home in the thick atmosphere of family solidarity, her ailments, which had started as rather temporary, ephemeral complaints, became more and more solid illness as mother and daughter fed their unconscious needs. Fanny was also drawn into the endless drama. As we have seen, she arranged appointments for Bella with the best London doctors in 1896; after that, whether because she wanted to spare her mother's anxiety, or because she had strong managerial talents, Fan took charge more and more of Bella's puzzling health. Bella was all set to return to Europe in January 1897 with Mrs. Arnold, a cousin. But Fan (visiting in New York at the time) wrote her the following:

> My dear Isabel—This family begs you before you decide on Europe just to try a homeopath, for they say that headaches are rather a specialty of homeos. Why not see Miss Fisher and find out whom she thinks well of. It may be worth while. Then Mrs. Lowell begs you to be hypnotized by Russell Sturgis before giving up hope in this country—and why not? Naturally, these dear people are greatly exercised over your health and when I descended to breakfast this morn, I found Mrs. Shaw and Mrs. Lowell combining in praises of homeopathy and quoting the case of Mr. Henry James to the purpose....

But Bella *did* manage to sail on the paquebot *Champagne* on January 16th, despite Fan's advice. And she sent off a note to her mother by the pilot, before even settling into her cabin: "My dearest darling Madam, Here I do be, with many really nice looking people; and one charming looking young man....I love you all and feel I am a Beast indeed to leave. No time for more. Your own Bol."

From her mid-twenties onward, Bella habitually spent months of each year away from her family, though she continued to write home faithfully—and of course her mother wrote to *her* daily, expressing great concern if a day or two went by without a letter from her daughter. She went to Europe again and again, often accompanied by one of her sisters or acting as a useful companion herself for an elderly cousin. Her letters written during these trips sparkle with amusing incidents and delightful people. In January 1904, she accompanied her elderly "Cousin A," having a wonderful time on shipboard, as there were several attractive (and attracted) young men on the steamer making its leisurely way via Gibraltar and Naples to Egypt. Isabella was then 32 years old, but the mother-child bond was still holding tight. Her first letter to her mother (written on the second day of the voyage) begins with a full page describing how poorly she felt, staying in her cabin all the first day, not seasick, but not wanting to bother to go up on deck. "I want my home and mother and pussycat, and my head aches. It hardly ached yesterday at all, I will add." But in the score and a half of subsequent letters she wrote on that trip, her maladies were never mentioned again. She was having a wonderful time, chatting and playing games with delightful ship-mates, marveling at awesome antiquities at Luxor, attending a very haute-monde ball at the British Embassy in Cairo where all the diplomats' and generals' chests were covered with medals.

"Cousin A" was Alice, oldest daughter of the poet Longfellow and Fanny Appleton Longfellow. After Fanny's tragic death, Hattie Appleton, her younger half-sister, spent much time caring for the Longfellow children, and the affectionate tie between "Aunt Hattie" and her motherless nieces and nephews remained strong long after Hattie married Greely Curtis and had a large family of her own. So it was only natural that Bella, uncomfortable and full of maladies at home, should stay with Cousin A for weeks and often months at a time. Cousin A was the only Longfellow daughter who never married. She lived alone in the great old house on Brattle Street in Cambridge and welcomed Bella's companionship there. But Bella's mother, just across the river in Boston, continued as usual to write her a daily letter or postcard, and Bella continued faithfully to respond, often throwing in some quick phrase about a roaring headache alongside an account of a splendid and delightful dinner party.

But Bella was not always away traveling, visiting distant friends or keeping company with Cousin A across the river during the winter months. A lot of the time she was right in the midst of her family, at 28 Mt. Vernon Street. And while her vigorous siblings went about their various civic and charitable causes, she was apt to go down the street to spend hours with her dear, but frequently bed-ridden friend, Alice Smith.

In the Victorian Era, semi-invalid maiden ladies were often found to be interesting and charming. Indeed, it was almost fashionable to frequent these invalids' chaises-longues, where their pathos only added to their charms, and afterwards to recount their conversation, rich with wisdom and brave humor.

We do not need to look back as far as Elizabeth Barrett Browning. Alice James, sister of Henry and William James, is an example. She was a contemporary of Bella Curtis and Alice Smith, though I do not know if the paths of the two Alices ever crossed in that dark age before Sigmund Freud brought enlightenment. Alice Smith lived with her sister Paulina and widowed mother and had a wide circle of admiring, sympathetic friends during the years she spent, increasingly disabled, in her bedroom. After her death, a book was privately printed containing many of her letters, her brightest sayings and her most profound observations. I came across a copy of this recently and tried to read it, hoping to understand the charm she spread among her healthy contemporaries, but soon laid it down, still mystified. Possibly an example of her wonderfulness appears in a letter from Fan Curtis to Bella, who was away travelling at a time when both Mrs. Smith and Paulina were critically ill with influenza. Fan had stopped by to inquire after the invalids and offer her help. She was met at the door by Alice, the chronic sufferer, whose first words of greeting were "Look at me! Am I not a miracle? I've been up all night, my hand in Paulina's!"

While growing up together, and well into their twenties, sister Fan, Elly, and Bella shared activities, confidences and endless jokes, and of course they wrote cozy letters to each other, whenever one was away:

Dec. 6th, 1891

> My darling Fangy, though tis nearly time
> For me to go to bed, I'll write to you in Rhyme
> And tell you all the topics of the day
> How once more Steenie's knee fell out in play
> How he a member of the Pudding is
> And all such light and merry little biz.
>
> But first I'll touch upon our Helly's woe
> (How could that brave young gent maltreat her so)
> She met him gay and giddy out this morn
> And he, with flattery to which manner born
> Did joke & say "Shall I you at home find

If I do call this aft?" Ah, what a cruel bind!
For she in pompous arrogance did wait
At home for him to call. Who was I now will state
That gay young blade so fast, so fresh and cool
Who makes our Elly play the doddering fool
His names abound in length: S.V.R.C.
So much for him. Now let us turn to me

I'm sick of this rhythm
And would now like to tell
How *my* flashy caller
Differs from Hell

He met me and said
If you do still thrive
May I come up and see you
At a half after five?

'Tis needless to state
That Helly wrote dirges
While I with my chatter
Amused Charley Sturgis.
                    I.C.
                    (Sunday eve, at half past nine,
                    Just the runcible hour to tell you a line.)

A year or so later, while off visiting in Cotuit, Fan was writing this to Bella:

> ...Here skirts and jackets is wore this season—and even sometimes these immaculate Codmans don't change for tea! I'm so glad not to be in that hole of a Boston tenanted by throngs of young men who come to call not on me, but only on you. (Ha?)

In the early '90s, Fan and Bella wrote many very affectionate and easy-going letters to each other; but by 1898, Fan was writing to Elly, "I wish Isabol wouldn't hang on to her ridiculous old heads like that—but still, her backaches having gone, I'm sure the heads will, pretty soon...." From then on, Fan took more and more charge of Bella's fluctuating maladies. After failing to get Bella interested in homeopathy, she urged her to go to an osteopath and even made an appointment with one before gaining Bella's consent. In fact, Fan's attitude toward Bella, though still affectionate, became increasingly managerial.

In 1908, psychotherapy, though not yet widely recognized as such, was beginning to be used as a valid approach to curing certain nervous disorders. Aunt Fan, ever concerned about her sister's complaints, persuaded Aunt Bog to enter a sanitarium in Bethel, Maine. To make sure she really carried through on this project, Fan accompanied Bella on the trip to Maine and stayed overnight to help her settle in. But it is obvious Bella resented Fan's high-handedness, for she sent her a rather sinister little poem later about a so-called loving sister who could banish her "to *dwell* in utmost misery at Bet*H E L L*." However, after her first week there, Bella began to accept the routine at Bethel and even came to enjoy some parts of it. Though her first letters to her mother were complaining and full of scorn, she presently began to write about some of her fellow-patients, both of their woes and their charms. She had a particularly good time, those crisply cold December mornings, chopping firewood with a Mr. Strong, while they laughed and sang together. As for the treatments, these consisted of regular private sessions with Dr. Gehring, during which he practiced what he called "Suggestion," which seems to have been a form of semi-hypnotism. He also required all his patients to retire to their rooms after lunch every day and rest on their right sides for half an hour.

This letter of December 10th to her mother shows that Dr. Gehring wanted new patients to get acclimatized before he began serious treatment:

Dearest Madam —
3 below zero at 7:30, as I ran over for breakfast this morning and 10 below in the night! But you never would suppose it, it is so very dry. You ask do the whistling winds hurt my head—there aint no wind. Its perfectly wonderful. And almost awesome the absolute stillness; and I wear a veil for my forehead 'tho don't really need it. Our sleighing party was so nice last night that this morn, with the doc's consent, I engaged a cutter and invited Mrs. Tilton to go with me, and we ambled gently

over to West Bethel through beautiful views—and on the return, ever shifting colors of sunset on the hills. She says she now can hardly wait for the "Suggestion" turn to come to me—Apparently one laughs or cries at first. But I don't look forward to it....The doc has given me a pot of bulbs for my window to tend, and I have planted the sweet smelling geraniums the Snellings sent, too. I slept pretty well last night but have felt rather meowsely today. You have never told me who Mrs. Bob Winsor was. She is now considered the Star Cure here—next to Dr. Mac Burney....

Several patients were discharged, totally cured, during Bella's stay at Bethel. But could any individual, already 36 years old, who continued to write a letter to her mother every day be cured by the "Suggestion" method? Of course Dr. Gehring couldn't succeed, since every professional session he held with Bella was described in her letters home, thus pocketing its significance. However, Bella stayed on at Bethel right through Christmas (missing the usual big family party) and for a number of weeks of treatment thereafter. When she returned home, she was much the same person as before. In March she went to Europe again, this time with her sister Hatty.

After another year (and another delightful European trip, this time with three lively friends) Bella went to Stockbridge to be cured by Dr. Austin Riggs, already well known as a successful therapist. His establishment was run like a private house rather than a sanitarium, and some half dozen people entangled in nervous disorders were under his care at a time. Here Bella ate three delicious meals a day, took brisk walks both morning and afternoon, and enjoyed the companionship of several other patients, well-heeled ladies of rather elite Boston and New York families. During the months of her stay in Stockbridge, she seems to have gained some insights about herself. She grew to admire Dr. Riggs, appreciate his acumen and enjoy his sense of humor. Moreover, she started a "Girls Club" for Stockbridge teenagers, and this entailed meetings with a variety of school and town officials, as well as members of old Stockbridge families.

As always, she wrote every single day to "Dearest Madam," and her mother kept every letter, marking on each envelope the date "I.C.Dec 5," "I.C.Dec 6"—all the way to I.C. March 27." The fat bundle of these, tied in blue ribbon, remains to this day, seventy-five years later. From them we get some clues of Austin Riggs' skillful and friendly practices. After three weeks at Stockbridge, Bella writes: "Dr. Riggs said today that there is nothing physically the matter with me—but he spoke of the headaches as real—I must change my attitude of mind. He thinks it's all right to continue wearing a veil over my head when out walking, though."

Dec. 28th. Spent the morning talking with a Mrs. Auchincloss, who is a great Episcopalian. We agree we both disagree with Dr. Riggs—a spiritually minded man, but mistaken.

Jan.6, 1911. I don't think you need worry about my getting too thin—we have gingerbread and cream every night! There's no strain here—save to remember to exaggerate *Nothing,* which comes hard!

Jan 10th [after a maid had chipped her goldfish bowl]. Dr. Riggs says I must cultivate a sense of humor about myself—that I must laugh at anybody else getting wrought up over a globe of minute fish being cracked by a half-witted cleaning woman—I guess he's right again, too!

Jan 18th. Dr. Riggs now orders mental arithmetic as a substitute for headache—for to multiply big numbers by 3 you *have* to visualize and concentrate and it is an excellent substitute... and it sure nuff is absorbing and works!

Jan 19th. Doc is now implying I may be cured by the end of February. He snorted when I mentioned April....

Jan 20th. Have had a real wouser of a headache, but intelligent Dr. R. knew just why—it was fear of *being sent home too soon.* He said he wouldn't yet awhile, and blamed himself....

Feb. 3rd. Said that bright-eyed young man this morning *Well,*, what's the matter with you? I've never seen your eyes so bright or your color so good—why you never could persuade *any* doctor that you weren't perfectly well! I said I'd had a good night and got up feeling extremely brisk and had been out walking with the thermo at 8, and felt fine and dandy, but didn't he think I'd be way down again tomorrow in consequence—he said sure, if you think you will be and plan according.

Alas, the therapy at Stockbridge, like that at Bethel, failed to produce a lasting effect. All those letters to "Dearest Madam" were, of course, read and discussed by the whole family, so that when Bella returned home, she was public property again, her need to be an independent individual subjected once more to jolly Curtis family solidarity. Presently everyone, including "Swashy" (the family doctor) agreed that Bella must surely have an actual physical growth in her head. Two years later, she was operated on by Harvey Cushing, the famous brain surgeon. Everybody was thrilled with the success of the operation, and Aunt Bog, when fully recovered, boasted to everyone that Dr. Cushing had removed a tumor "the size of a walnut" from inside her skull. Actually, he had found no tumor and nothing whatever the matter, Dr. Cushing told my husband (also a doctor) when they met at a medical meeting some years later.

The year between her Stockbridge cure and her brain operation, however, was a particularly lively and interesting one for Aunt Bog. In the winter of 1912, Jim Curtis, then Undersecretary of the Treasury, had some official business to carry out concerning the Panama Canal, then under construction. He took along on the trip his sisters Bella and Hatty, going first by train to New Orleans, stopping off en route for a few days of quail-shooting on a friend's plantation.

New Orleans, January 13, 1912

Dearest Madam. What a victory! We are more and more excited over it. We got the Herald last night and just couldn't believe it. Well well well now I hope Mr. Moors is not dead nor Joe neither and that Susy Fitz is quieted for good. So be it. But of course you really want to hear of our experiences—for i' faith, I have not written a letter since just before quail shooting with Pansy. Also, will you deposit for me my dividends promptly as I see that travelling en prince—prince say I. Vive l'empereu—will be a-going some, and I can cash a cheque most any old where. To go back to Tuesday—We had the perfect day, the first for three weeks without rain they said, and we thoroughly enjoyed it. The bird dogs, the trainer, the boy, the horses and mules all in turn being of use in the hunting. Then, in some mysterious way, a sit-down hot lunch at tables was served in the depths of the wood by Davidson (butler) and a negro understudy. After which Hat rode with Pansy (of course saddle horses appeared too) and I drove with Miss Thomas through woods and along the lake and home for tea.

Sat morn the 13th, continued
(On board United Fruit Co's S.S. Atenas)

And I'd hardly got started quail shooting when we were hustled to the boat and now they say the pilot or whatever goes in an hour and this can go then. And MY! you should see our suite! Hat and I have brass beds and private bath. Also Mrs. and Miss Wadsworth opposite—and now appears a Customs Official with candy.

But back back back to Horseshoe: Thursday morning we drove many miles to see Pansy's cotton ginned but though it was there and ready twas not to be done until the next day—but presently in a neighboring wood appeared our lunch, as on the day before, and just as we finished up came the motor with all our goods aboard and into Tallahassee we went over road that beggars description....In New Orleans we walked the town, old French quarter etc, and at lunch appeared Jim, Elliott Wadsworth & Basil. In the afternoon we went to make a Social Call at the Custom House all of us, that is Jib, Elliott, Hat and I, as Jib didn't want to have it official. And MY! Such bowing and salaaming. It was very amusing (and now have just appeared two officials with candy for us!) After that we went to see the old Slave Market and such and then for tea. To dinner (on Elliott) at the most unctuous-fooded spot in the French Quarter ever you put tooth to....

The Wadsworths seem chatty and friendly Mrs. being fat and roly poly he looks about 18 and has been Speaker of the Assembly! is aged about 34. Harriet nice looking and fair haired with Basil in close attendance I opine....

Well dearest Madam,

We have seen and shaken hands with the great man—perhaps you may not realize that there is only *one* Great Man in the world —and Goethals is his name. It is distinctly amusing to be treated as great folks ourselves, but Jim or mayhap twas Elliott says the social end is considered very important that everybody is to go home saying the canal is the Greatest Thing in the world. Be that as it may, a little motor car for the railroad tracks met us at Culebra and we whirled down and in and through and round the cut. Really, my dear Madam, it is marvelous—phenomenal. And perfectly thrilling. And until you've seen it and the 35000 laborers working it you can never believe the magnitude of the job or the speed with which it is being done. Then we went by appointment to the Administration building to meet the Col. and first a man explained on a chart and raised map all the details of the Canal & a little working plan of the locks. Then we were called into the office, introduced to a very genial pleasant-eyed man who promptly hoped we'd enjoyed our trip through the cut. And then said for tomorrow you'd like to go to the Gatun Dam, Monday see the Pacific and Tuesday go on the trip to see our island—Wednesday be shown the reconstructed rail-way—You leave Thursday? You have a railroad pass? Does it include all your party? A few more words and out. Supplemented this eve by Col. Cook, who has done everything for us so far, by having a Gov. rig to take us on Sunday to Old Panama, seven miles away, where we plan to spend the day.

Yesterday was the grand celebration of the Chinese Republic and there was lots doing for there be thousands of chinks in this country....Today we just rebbered the morn, and Jib Hat and I drove out to Balboa where the Canal comes out at this end. Our trip tomorrow starts at 6:30 A.M.!...

What a lively and interesting trip that was! And how extraordinary that only a few months later the whole family, Bella included, should decide that she ought to have a brain operation!

But Bella was not incapacitated, even at home, though her maladies kept recurring, off and on. In fact she lived actively and healthily much of the time. Like her sisters, she was engaged in good works, though perhaps not so strenuously as they. In the winter season, when the family was settled in town, she worked regularly at the Boston Dispensary, organizing patients' files in the record room. But her chief occupation over many years was promoting interest and support for Penn School. This educational, agricultural and industrial centre was on St. Helena Island, off the coast of South Carolina, where many freed slaves' families had been abandoned by their former masters following the Civil War. Aunt Bog was devoted to Penn School. She raised money for it, she collected cast-off clothes for it, and winter after winter she went to stay on the island for six or more weeks at a time. Here she was welcomed by its administrators, Rossa Cooley and Grace House, who became her very good friends. She helped them out, wherever and whenever she could, in daily chores, and they all enjoyed these visits together. And they all loved dogs. Rossa and Grace owned Shetland Collies and gave one to Bella.

Up to now I have said nothing about Aunt Bog's dogs. Starting with birds and kittens, and moving on to dogs and goldfish, she lavished affection on a succession of pets. For years, "Teaka," a yellow mongrel, was her constant companion. After that came three generations of Old English Sheepdogs. "Raggie," the matriarch of these, produced Robin, General Joffre, Ursula and Joanna. Joanna gave birth to thirteen puppies one morning, while taking a walk with Aunt Bog along the shore path. We young nieces talked about this for days, and how Aunt Bog had to retrace her steps along her route, to be sure she hadn't missed any squirmy little poppet behind a stone or under a fern. We also spent hours over at the Aunts' house, admiring Joanna and her brood in their pen. But of course Aunt Bog didn't keep all those puppies. They were all dispensed with to friends or buyers except General Sir Douglas Haig, who, shaggy and long-haired, galumphed beside Aunt Bog on her daily walks for many years, answering to the affectionate nickname of

Mrs. Nathan Appleton
(née Harriot Coffin Sumner)
(1802-1867)

Nathan Appleton
(1779-1861)

Isabella Stevenson Curtis,
wife of James
(1805-1880)

James Freeman Curtis
at age 29
(1797-1839)

28 Mt. Vernon St., the upper hall

Two views of the Manchester house

Swimming at the Bathing Rocks

In the stable lived the four horses; in winter, cows kept them company; pigs lived underneath; hay and onions were stored in the loft above.

All the children, c. 1887

Playing cards on the terrace, 1892

On the porch, 1892

Greely and his children on "The Dream," c. 1885

Mrs. Greely S. Curtis

Aunt Fan in her Paris gown, c. 1886

Aunt Hat, c. 1895

Aunt Bog, c. 1905

Aunt Pedge, c. 1921

Aunt Bog at Moon Island

The Family Next Door...
Elinor Curtis Hopkinson with her artist husband Charles,
and their five daughters (from l. to r.) Happy, Elly, Joany, Ibby, Maly

Aunt Pedge, c. 1903

Aunt Hat, c. 1905

Photograph of the Curtis Sisters in
The Boston Sunday Globe, *May 15, 1960*

'Aigy. After the sheepdog dynasty came the series of Shetland collies. The first one was definitely Aunt Bog's personal pet, but after that all the Aunts got into the act and became loving parents. It was not in the Curtis code ever openly to express affection for each other, and the Aunts never did so. But it was all right to pour out love on dogs—to cuddle them and spoil them, to give them treats between meals, to show off their clever tricks to visitors, and tell long anecdotes of their intelligence while hugging them. The Aunts' Shetland collies were high-strung little creatures; if they heard the rattle of a latch, they would rush to the front door, snarling and barking hysterically, and sometimes even biting the incoming caller, be it friend or stranger. But the Aunts totally ignored these vicious outbursts. Their little darlings could do no wrong.

With summer came real happiness for Aunt Bog. She owned an island, and here she was queen of a magical domain. Back at the turn of the century, when staying with Cousin A at Holderness, New Hampshire, on the shore of Lake Asquam, Bella Curtis had explored this island by canoe. She paddled around it, noticing its many little beaches, its dark groves of hemlock and pine, its charming silver birches and luxuriant high-bush blueberries. There were no buildings, and no human voices to be heard. In 1904 she bought it, and christened her paradise "Moon Island." A camp of rough boards was built that first summer, and this remained unaltered for the next forty years. It consisted of a big central room with fireplace, three little bedrooms each equipped with two cots and a door opening out into the forest, and a small kitchen with a diminutive wood-burning stove. There was no running water; a pump outside the kitchen door drew water from the lake, to fill the pails—two big enamel ones for the kitchen, three smaller ones for the bedroom wash-stands. There was no electricity, no telephone, no communication with the outside world except the mail boat, which came every day at noon, bringing that unfailing letter from Mother Curtis, and frequent food supplies—fresh eggs from the Manchester hens, milk and fruits from a shoreside grocery store.

Bella was never alone on the island. Relatives and friends

took turns staying with her, in well-planned succession. As soon as her nephews and nieces were old enough to know how to swim, they became her enthusiastic companions. "Oh why did we have to leave that palace of delight?" moaned Happy and Maly, my two older sisters, on returning from their first visit. Home at Manchester, with its tiresome electricity, maids, telephone and the whole Atlantic Ocean in front of it seemed humdrum and shabby compared to that rough-hewn camp Aunt Bog inhabited. The next year, when I was seven years old, I was allowed to go to the Island for a week's visit. Everything was perfect. Aunt Bog had a set routine for carrying through a variety of daily chores, and we happily followed her rules. She had names for everything, too. The little wood stove, already labeled "Dotty" by its manufacturer, required that "Dotty-food" be sawed every day, to cook all meals; and the wood to be sawed had to be collected by scouting through the forest for fallen branches, and lugging them back to the camp. The big yellow thermometer hanging on a piazza post was named "Old Mustard;" even the scenic Italian dinner plates had names. ("Aigy and the Loons" was the favorite). A crudely carved matchbox container was called "Mr. Brooks's Stomach." I never knew the origin of this last appellation, but always hoped it had something to do with an early romance. Could the whittler have been an earnest admirer of Aunt Bog?

All the beaches and paths on the Island had names, too. To get to "Edna-Maude" beach, you walked along the "Romany Patteran," so-named for the many Gypsy moth nests found on its bordering trees. "Birch Boulevard" naturally ended at "Birch Boulevard Beach," and another good swimming place was reached by strolling down "Crossed-in-Lovers Lane," a path originally hacked out of the forest by two maiden ladies then past their prime, but retaining their sense of humor.

The day began for us as soon as we heard the coffee-grinder. This meant that Aunt Bog had already returned from her swim at the Bathing Beach, where a cake of Ivory Soap was kept on a rock rising out of the shallow water of the cove, its sandy bottom dimpled with golden discs from the early-rising sun.

There was a bench and rack beside the water, and here we stripped off our pajamas to plunge in for the first swim of the day. Every morning seemed like the beginning of the world and we the first mortals taking part in its creation, as we swam out toward the rising sun, the gentle water sliding by our bare skin, the dark and silent trees behind us.

Breakfast was ready for us when we returned. One of Aunt Bog's firmest rules was that she cook all meals and wash all dishes; guests then dry all dishes, and put them away. This ceremony was always accompanied by jokes and laughter—though each dish had to be returned to its exact place on the shelf, and each spoon to its own pre-designated slot. But the routine chores at the Island never seemed tiresome or arduous. Filling pails, sawing dotty-food, cleaning lamp-chimneys and sweeping the big room were all easily executed because all were part and parcel of Aunt Bog's happy concept of how to live self-sufficiently on an island. How she enjoyed this life! And its magic spread to all her visitors. Living on an island only a mile in circumference, stripped from the clutter of modern "conveniences," one returns to the essentials. One is both subject to and an integral part of elemental nature. It is challenging and exhilarating; living for days or weeks at a time cut off from the world brings forth necessarily self-reliance and ingenuity. Some people painted landscapes, some wrote poetry, some turned to carpentry. Uncle Steen invented a way of telling time accurately. A ray of sunlight, shining through a hole he had bored in the roof, penetrated the living room, causing a bright sun-image (the size of a shirt button) to move along the floor as the day progressed. This spot crossed a line painted on the floor at *exactly noon* every day. The line was curved to harmonize with the earth's elliptical orbiting of the sun, and Sundays were marked off by thumbtacks placed along the line in diminishing proximity to each other as the season rolled from June to September and the days shortened.

The gentle lapping sound of the lake was always beckoning us mortals, young and old, to step in for a swim, and this everyone did three or four times a day. The water was deliciously sympathetic—not too cold, but not soupily warm, either. We stayed in for ages, sometimes swimming a purposeful Australian crawl, sometimes an indolent breast-stroke, and often just floating on our backs looking up at the sky. Swimming off the wharf, near the camp, was always fun because at its further end was a springboard, slanting out over deep water, and encouraging old and young to make fantastic dives and somersaults. Swimming at Edna-Maude or Birch Boulevard Beach was equally delightful, but in a far more tranquil way. To reach these, we'd wander down the Island clad in bathing suits and usually carrying a basket, in case we came across a particularly prolific blueberry patch. Aunt Bog made wonderfully satisfying blueberry muffins, and her guests gorged on them throughout the berry season.

The high-bush blueberries, however, flourished close to the shoreline, and these were more fun to approach by water. These bushes were so generously fruited that you could pick a quart in no time, by "milking" clusters of berries with one hand into a container held by the other, while the boat rocked gently to and fro in the shallow water. The boat was named "Mr. Skiffington," a row-boat with thwarts for two rowers. The Red Canoe, however, was even better for berry-picking, as it could glide nearer to shore. Aunt Bog had two canoes; the green one, "Tippy," was unsuitable for obvious reasons, but the red one was entirely trustworthy, and long enough to carry four people: two paddlers at bow and stern and two passengers sitting comfortably on cushions amidships. It was almost impossible to tip over, no matter how hard you tried. Nobody knows how long Cousin A had owned the Red Canoe before she gave it to Aunt Bog when the latter first occupied Moon Island, the summer of 1904. Seventy-nine years later, it was still reliable when I paddled around the Island in it, though there was a small leak near the bow. This sturdy relic remains a monument to the loving care given to every essential on the Island by its owner. Though unskilled paddlers had gashed it time and again on sharp rocks, Aunt Bog patched its gaping wounds, and re-painted the Red Canoe again and again.

Swimming and boating, chopping trees and sawing wood gave Island visitors plenty of exercise, but there was always plenty of time besides for simply lounging on the piazza, reading and chatting, with the lake's changing aspects ever before us—a dazzling glitter in a breeze, a magic mirror in a calm. Way across the water to the west, beyond the "Three Sisters" Islands, the Rattlesnake Mountains rose from the mainland. To the Southeast, beyond the tip of "Great Island," and too far away to see was a cove where great blue herons nested in ancient trees. We were always planning to visit this heronry on some calm day, by canoe. But it was so delightful swaying gently in the Gloucester hammock on the piazza, one's reading interrupted from time to time by loons laughing to each other somewhere out there in the water, that we never made the expedition. Besides loons, there were many warblers, nuthatches and woodpeckers, and owls would call at night. Occasionally an eagle soared overhead, and every year there was a new family of mergansers. "Mrs. Merganser" would sail by, followed by a parade of obedient babies —sometimes nine or ten, sometimes even twelve dark little forms prudently keeping in Indian file behind her.

By mid-August, when the nights grew colder and mosquitoes were no longer a scourge, we pulled our cots outdoors, under the open sky, and watched for shooting stars until we went to sleep, to sleep soundly until awakened by the rackety chirruping of a red squirrel, enthusiastically starting his day in the big pine tree near the sleeping piazza.

Long before bedtime, before it was time to go indoors and light the kerosene lamp, came a serene and lovely interval. The last supper-dish having been washed and put away, the day's work was over for Aunt Bog, and she joined us on the big piazza to sit and watch the sunset. She was totally relaxed. While the afterglow grew crimson in the west, making black silhouettes of the Rattlesnake mountains, she would reminisce and philosophize, and we would join in, our voices made gentle by the mysterious beauty around us. She talked of old happenings and of new ideas, with wisdom, affectionate humor and keen observation, and we all felt free to express our own opinions.

For half a century Aunt Bog reigned over her magic kingdom. But alas, as old age crept up on her, it brought with it crippled limbs; no longer able to climb in and out of boats, stroll down woodland paths or swim off a favorite beach, she gave up her beloved island to spend summer days at Manchester, sitting on a balcony facing the sea.

But "The Island" lived on. All the rules and regulations, the customs and the names for paths and beloved objects were kept alive by its new owner, Uncle Steen's daughter, Fanny Ham, "Finny." Like all Aunt Bog's nephews and nieces, she had always loved staying on Moon Island for a week or two every summer since she was seven years old, and now she and her husband Hale and their children made it their summer home and made it flourish once again. It was a joy to visit them and find all Aunt Bog's special lares and penates intact; except for a motor-boat and a few other modernities, they had made time stand still.

It is all gone now. No trace of the camp remains—not a chair, not a plate, a canoe or a spoon; not a bed or a hatchet, a hammock or a saucepan. In 1984, when the summer season was over and everyone had left, a fierce thunderstorm swept over the Island. A bolt of lightning struck the camp. The towering flames of the burning building were soon seen from the mainland, and men set out in speedboats. But by the time they reached the Island campsite, they found nothing but smoldering embers. One relic still remains, however—the Island's Guest Book. Luckily, Fin and Hale had taken it with them for safe-keeping when they left at the end of the summer. This historic volume is inscribed with the names of scores of happy visitors, interspersed with their drawings, witticisms and poetry. A splendid example of this last, written by our cousin Edith Standen, is displayed herewith:

VERSES FOR AUNT BOG ON HER SEVENTY-FIFTY BIRTHDAY

Three quarters of a century ago,
As Jupiter was wand'ring here below
He came upon the naiad of Squam Lake
A-blubbering as if her heart would break.

"What ails thee, wat'ry nymph?" the monarch cried
As tenderly her weeping orbs he dried.
She sobbed and spoke "Among my islands fair
The loveliest still lacks the proper care,
Disfigured by a coarse, plebeian name,
All tangled, rough and ugly! To my shame
I cannot find an underling so fit
That I can trust her to look after it."
"Be of good cheer," far-seeing Jove decreed,
"A mortal has been chosen for this deed.
A babe is born at Manchester this night,
And Isabella Curtis is she hight."

Prophetic rapture seized the naiad then,
She laughed upon the king of gods and men.
"I see it all!" she cried, "The bathing beach,
With soap convenient to the bather's reach,
The piles of dotty-food, the wharf so strong,
Upturned canoes all neatly ranged along;
The paths so trim, yet never artificial
The tree carved o'er with everyone's initial!
Moon Island she a Paradise shall make,
The brightest jewel of my silver lake!"

E.A.S. October 25, 1947

Is it possible that Jupiter himself destroyed Aunt Bog's camp? After all, lightning bolts were his favorite weapons. Did he and that rather emotional naiad feel that no other human could ever take the place of their hand-picked Island Queen?

It is a mercy that Aunt Bog never knew of this disaster, the sudden annihilation of what she had held so dear; she had died long before the catastrophe.

In her later years, she became reconciled to living at home with her sisters. Though she still lashed out at them with fierce remarks, nobody took these seriously. I certainly didn't, that time I brought her a photograph in a dear little Florentine frame. It was of her favorite and most sympathetic sister Elly, my mother. "Perfectly hideous!" she exclaimed, and handed it back to me. I knew she was really very pleased, and we settled down for a nice chat.

She had always loved her Manchester home, and in her earliest years had always been the first Curtis to move down from Boston in the spring and the last to move back to town in the autumn. In fact, she often had stayed on in that great cold stone house well into December. That was when we nieces were children, and I well remember keeping her company there overnight, and trying to help her get breakfast the next morning. No water flowed from the kitchen pump, and the dish towels hanging above it were frozen stiff as boards. In her later years, she was more devoted to "Manch" than ever. After giving up Moon Island, she had a decade of good long-drawn-out summer seasons there, before being relegated to a wheel chair. Almost every morning she walked over to the Hopkinson House, to "pass the time of day" with her "Sister Hop" (Elly), and the two sisters would sit together talking and laughing in wicker chairs out on the lawn. If it was a cold autumn morning, they sat indoors where my father had already got logs going in the big living-room fireplace. "It's easy to see its his mother-in-law's wood he's burning," she snarled, as she sat down to be comfortable in its warmth one morning. Father smiled serenely, knowing that tangled up in barbed wire was a perfectly good heart of gold.

Though none of the Curtis sisters had a college education, Aunt Bog was very well read, and in her later years she remained an avid reader. She kept up with current affairs through the *Atlantic Monthly*, the *Nation*, *Punch* and the daily papers, and she wrote letters to the *Transcript* under the pseudonym of "Angela Street." She also held an important post in the Curtis sisters' household, for she managed the joint account they maintained to cover their mutual living expenses. She was a fastidious bookkeeper, and the other three all relied on her accuracy and fairness.

Accuracy played no part in her typewriting skills, however. She had acquired a machine in the 1920s, and through the ensuing decades she recklessly typed out single-spaced lines covering every inch of a standard 8 x 11 sheet of paper with exotic spelling and punctuation, while writing to any of her sisters who was absent from home. Hat and Pedge were both abroad when she wrote this, from "28," in Boston:

Dear Girls,

Peg's from Paris of Feb 25th, and from Warsaw both came to paw on Saturday. Would say they read real interesting....Friday we had the tea for Maria and Mrs. Cleghorn, and I must say it was one of Francie's masterpieces. The two beneficiaries arrived at 4:30 Francie blowing in from her bowl shop at quarter of five, explained that she hadn't asked any guests until five (having asked them at four-thirty) and trotted upstairs to change her clothes. (I of course couldn't change mine, as Steen was holding a long session with Miss Lee in my room.) And there were present I may say the job-lotest. We only lacked the Thatchers, Nichols and Lulu Guild to be perfect. Francie swears she invited some of our high-grade friends, but the nearest approach to it were Dixey, Tappan and Maudie. Yes sirs, It was a party! Our pretty little Theresa, knowing nothing of the ways of the house, having to answer the doorbell, fished out the strangest uneven cups and plates, and I think hid most of the time in the laundry closet. What Maria and Mrs. Cleghorn thought of it I can't imagine but it certainly was the darndest!...Little Dicky, to dinner here yesterday announced that the way to get married was to have a girl in a white dress.

> *Well, no more at present,*
> *Mrs. Myron C. Wick*

Why sign herself off as Mrs. Myron C. Wick? Mrs. W.'s significance is now long lost in antiquity, but doubtless was a family byword at the time.

Aunt Bog never failed to send out an annual appeal for funds for Penn School, every winter, when the family was in town. Here she is writing to Aunt Hat about the great task:

January 26, 1931

And so here it is Sunday eve again, and I most too tired to tinkle the types, we have had kind friends and fellow workers here from 10 am till 6:45 when I went to take my bath. However they did do a doos of a heap of work and about 5000 Penn reports have been folded, ready to be folded for the last time and put with eleven thousand other things into a tight cheap envelope and I am perfectly sure no one will bother to even open them, this year we are typing Dear Mrs. Speddiddle-fish (or Mr.) which adds enormously to the job and I've bout 2000 more to do, having spent Friday, Sat and all 'smorn doing that. Francie left Friday morn, up to her ears with meetings till the last gunfire....

She also managed to give their Old English sheepdog a bath.

...and yesterday was the good old fashioned snow storm beginning Friday eve and continuing till noon yesterday, and cars skidding hither and yon. Yes, and a bath for Haigy last night!!! He actually had one, but not so absolutely spotless as usual as he lay down in the tub and refused to stir so I had to sorter wash round him, always with the fear that his nose might go under and he not pull it up! and when it came to getting him out again he refused to stir, "You put me in, now take me out if you want to" was his very distinct utterance, w'ich perforce I had to do. Peg had her favorite little Hunter friend here to dine and go to the concert, so before they went they began on him, and he is to all intents and purposes dry now....Have *you* got my old sleevelinks, the ones with black squiggly lines on gold????? I can't find them at all, and must go to Manch to see if they're there.

Nuff said

Aunt Bog's letters from "Manch" were sagas of all that was happening on the estate, from the health of cows and vegetable garden to the comings and goings of nephews and nieces. We five Hopkinson nieces received a lot of attention in these epics, partly because, living alongside of the Aunts, we were omnipresent in the "Manch" scene, but perhaps also because for these four spinster women we were surrogate children. Happy (or Hap), Maly, Ibby, Elly and Joany appear again and again in Aunt Bog's letters. By the time we five girls were in our late teens and twenties, the Aunts were almost as interested in the young men that frequented our house as we were ourselves. Were we now surrogates in another way, a way that had always been denied them? The following letter is a fairly good sample of

108

"auntly" interest. It was written by Aunt Bog to her sister Hat in October 1930, a few weeks before my marriage to Jim Halsted. The letter is so long that I'll spare the reader the quarter of it dealing with dogs, another Penn School mailing and a marvelous crop of seckel pears.

...Now for the Hops: Ib and Jim have practically taken a tinny winny apt at 100 Chestnut St next to Lena Hardy's but yesterday Sue and Bill Herman came down and urged them to look at one next door to them, so perhaps they will. You should see all the advertisements etc. that por in the last being a lady in an absolute wedding style, two envelopes, and requesting the pleasure of helping Miss Hopkinson in any way she could, mentioning—all engraved, mind you—from every detail to planning the wedding trip!!!!! Maria is going with keen interest and joy to Jones' in London to get the rest of the table silver that we are giving. Joany went to the football game with Bill Stix, looking very charming, Maly poured tea at "Uncle" Freddy Cabot's party for the Henschels and went to the Concert with F.G. and they drove home in M's open car with Frances Sturgis just as the wind rose furiously and the thermo began to drop. ...Then Hap and Elly in a twitter worst confounded had a beau from the steamer going over who has corresponded with them ever since, Abbott Hamilton by name from N.Y. about 30, Princeton, and owns a yacht in which he raced to Bermuda, and elsewhere, so wonder of wonders he sounds well to do! They brought him over to tea yester aft, and have blown through here off and on all day winding up with tea again, Elly positively delirious, I never have seen her so eager and excited. But first this morning quite early appeared Ibby and Jim, simply raging with Happy for letting Maly step in and snatch him away from Elly with not a sound—(it transpires that he and Maly met at a late breakfast, and to listen to Ibb it would sound as tho' it were premeditated!) too comic. And then when Maly came to tea she said "Why you never saw anyone so wild as Elly about him, we met at breakfast and sat and chatted and you'd suppose I was out to vamp him from them all, just because we sat and ate fishballs together for why it must have been at least 20 minutes."...Certain Teddy Hayward was a quiet little piece in comparison with the whirlwind effect as El, Hap Hamilton Stix followed slowly by Joany and Ibb and Jim to play pingpong after dinner setting the radio going at its loudest and jazziest to dance as they played. So I upstakes and went over to their house and no sooner was settled to chat with their Ma than most of the troupe reappeared all but Elly & Stix with whom she had to play tennis against her desires "so silly of her when he is obviously Happy's beau" said Maly as she and Frances discussed them at tea....

Aunt Bog's garden, at Manchester, was beautiful, and tending it was her life-long occupation and pleasure. It was a pleasure for all of us. Set in a hollow, and thus protected from savage salt seawinds and cold blasts from the Northwest, it was a charming bright-flowering little area of formality amidst the wild and casual outgrowths of nature surrounding it. There were neat rectangular flowerbeds with brick-edged paths between them. In the centre was a three-tiered Venetian fountain, rising from a pool where goldfish dashed and idled among waterlilies. There was a bench to sit on and enjoy the roses and delphiniums, the lilies and lupin and all the annuals Aunt Bog planted each spring. As children we sat there in amazement, to watch a spinning ping-pong ball cling to the column of water spouting skyward from the fountain.

In her later years, Aunt Bog no longer transplanted as many annuals, but she still spent happy hours in her garden. She weeded the flowerbeds, and every spring she cleaned out the winter's debris of dead leaves from the empty pool before turning on the fountain again to refill it, and liberating her goldfish to frisk once more among the waterlily plants. (They had spent the winter in a glass bowl in Boston.)

But gardening became too trying for her arthritis, and Aunt Bog's daily walks grew shorter and shorter, and she depended more heavily on her cane. By the time she was in her eighties, the stairs became too tiring to maneuver, and she lived entirely on the second floor of the big Manchester house. Luckily, there was a balcony, and she trundled out in her wheel chair to sit here for many hours each day. Though she did some knitting and reading, it was good to just sit facing the sea, watching the waves creaming whitely against Dana Island, listening to the seagulls, and keeping an eye out for anybody walking up from the shore path through the lawn below. Overhead, the clouds glided and grouped or vanished in the eternity of sky.

As she approached the age of ninety, her mind seemed as sharp as ever, but her body began to fail her woefully, and her sisters, deciding it was too difficult to provide proper care for her, put her in a nursing home. Exiled from everything she loved, everything that was familiar and dear to her, her mind became more and more disoriented until she died in 1966, in her ninety-fifth year.

There are many enigmas in my mind when I think about Aunt Bog. Certainly, of the four Curtis sisters, she was the least involved in public life. While Fan, Hat and Peg were all outstanding for their accomplishments in what was still a man's world, she was the noticeable exception. Her sisters strode heartily and successfully into golf tournaments and committee meetings, while she sat at home sharing laughter and sympathy with intimate friends. Now, rather than scorning her for eccentricities, hot temper and lack of public deeds, I'd like to give her a very loving hug. But what would she say if I did?

Aunt Hat, c. 1905

Chapter Six

Aunt Hat

Harriot Sumner Curtis 1881-1974

Why did Aunt Hat behave without promoting her own ego, as her sisters did? Perhaps it began with her nose. She was born with a large, aquiline nose, dominating all her other features— so noticeably that her mother's friends, writing congratulations on the birth of the ninth Curtis baby, added consolations. As a little child she was very aware of her nose, she once told me, and ashamed of her looks. And those teasing, rollicking big brothers of hers never let her forget it. The need to be inconspicuous while joining in family games may have launched her on a long life of useful activities unobstructed by self-promotion. Aunt Fan basked happily in the glow of public approval; Aunt Bog's ego, fluctuating between charm and ferocity, was seldom out of sight; Aunt Pedge told long stories of her own exploits; but Aunt Hat went about her various concerns with a modesty that enabled her to see clearly the gist of a current matter and where she might usefully lend a hand. She was not a talker, but a doer.

When Miss Dewar, the manager of the Maverick Dispensary, was disabled temporarily, Aunt Hat dashed over to East Boston to take over the reception desk, thus freeing the assistant manager to take Dewar's place. [1] When Hampton Institute was short-handed, Aunt Hat went down to Virginia to "pinch-hit" (she called it) as Dean of Women; she stayed there four years.

---

[1] The Maverick Dispensary had been established years earlier to provide out-patient medical service in East Boston for the then surging Italian-American population. Aunts Hat and Pedge kept the dispensary going for years, soliciting donations from their friends to maintain its staff.

When her brother Jim was going through the turmoil of divorce, Aunt Hat was at his side in Paris during the exhausting legal proceedings, and afterwards in Italy, where she helped his children to adjust and learn to live without their mother, in a villa Jim temporarily rented outside Florence.

I like to remember how she taught me to swim, for this, like her other deeds, was done without personal fanfare. She didn't say, "Now watch me—do this with your hands—don't be afraid —I'll hold you up, etc." She said, "Let's lie down here, where the water is shallow." I was a little fat five-year-old then. We lay face down, side-by-side, our heads facing the land, our feet seawards, our arms outstretched. Only our stomachs were resting on the sandy bottom. The sea was fairly calm that day, and the waves were slow and gentle. The first one only sloshed around me, but the second one was bigger: it picked me right up and carried me, floating, way up onto the beach. Floating! I was floating! It was magic. The sea wasn't an enemy, it was my friend, and I could swish my arms and kick my legs and move myself along, too, because the *water would hold me up*. From then on I was never afraid. By her deliberate self-effacement, Aunt Hat had given me self-reliance.

Aunt Hat was also a very good athlete. She was an ardent little player on the Curtis Family baseball team in her early years, and later an enthusiastic tennis player, most cooperative as a doubles partner. As for golf, she and Pedgy were indefatigable. They got their start at the Essex County Club, as little girls, when it first opened. By their late teens, they were playing in tournaments up and down the Eastern Seaboard. Pedgy was competitive enough for two and had even qualified for the Women's National Golf Championship when she was a thirteen year old. Hat, though vivacious and high-spirited, was never egotistically aggressive. She loved playing her best and was the winner of several tournaments. She and Pedge soon began playing tournament golf further afield; they played in Cleveland and Chicago, in England and Ireland. Back at home, the Curtis family read the newspapers' sports pages avidly, for "the Curtis Sisters" were becoming well-known. Whenever either of the girls won, they were showered with telegrams and congratulatory notes from their devoted mother and siblings; if they were defeated, commiserations followed. Hat and Pedge, however, played better and better golf. They were playing in a tournament in Morristown, New Jersey, in 1905 when Hat wrote home about the prowess of the "Kid" (Pedgy):

Friday Eve.

I verily believe you all are one degree more excited than we. She has played crackajack golf all the week and if she continues to get off long balls will have Pauline pressing into every ditch and railroad track. There are a good half dozen holes that Kid is the only one to be able to reach in two or three....Pauline did play better than I've ever seen her—drat her. Still, I think we're still coming. A 41 today is a record. Here are some cuttings I think are good—the N.Y. Herald has a sporting editor who knows....

The next year it was Hat who triumphed: the Winner of the National Women's Golf Championship was Harriot S. Curtis!!! She was closely followed by Pedgy, who in 1907 became National Champion, winning the title from her own sister, for Hat was her opponent in the final match.

Aunt Hat's delight in sports began long before golf became so absorbing. Besides her agility on the family baseball team at Manchester, there were all those games to play in winter, in the backyard of 28 Mt. Vernon St. Among the neighboring children who came to skate and play games there was Margaret Nichols. "Pickles" Nichols and Hatty became fast friends, and Hatty often spent a week or two with the Nichols family in the summers at their place in New Hampshire. "We're having great sport," she writes home to Mama, "tennis, baseball, golf, swimming, and just fooling around...." These sound like good interests for athletic children, but by her late teens, one might expect Hatty to sound more feminine, more interested in the opposite sex. But no: telling of last night's supper party of two girls and five boys, she writes Mama, "The boys are all bully," and goes on to say she is "having a corking old time. Going over to the Kennedy's Thursday afternoon was bully—their place is just like a club, with 2 tennis courts, a bully links and a pool with boats—even a swan boat."

Though Hatty was an attractive young woman with a good figure, beautiful understanding eyes and an outgoing nature, she seems never to have thought of herself as a desirable female; she never appears to have had or sought any deeper relationship with a man than playing tennis with him as a partner or going skating if he asked her—but only if another skater came along, too. Apparently, when young, she used to say, "He's a boy—I hate him," quite frequently. But at a house party at Putnam Camp in the Adirondacks when she was nineteen, she had become more tolerant. "There are lots of young men," she writes, "and all very nice. Langdon Warner is *very* pleasant.... I'm afraid I'm getting a very swelled head, because I keep winning at crokinole and cribbage....Last night everyone had to draw a portrait of somebody else, and I did one of Langdon with his flaming red hair and orange eyebrows. Everybody recognized him at once. There are no 'cases' unless you count Dr. Hewes doing a certain amount of chasing after Ellen Bellows...." In spite of Langdon's attention, it is obvious that Hatty remained a spectator, rather than a participant in romance. And so she continued.

Except for men, her enthusiasms were many. She loved food of all kinds; she loved flowers. She marveled at sunsets, and when the moon was full, she always stepped outdoors at night to wonder at it and the moonpath across the water. She had a flower garden of her own, there at Manchester, beside the house, and when one of her favorite rosebushes was all abloom, she would stand before it, clippers in hand, giving exclamations of loving admiration before cutting off a few perfect flowers to decorate the living room. When out for a walk, she carried the clippers along to cut back scratchy cat-briar sprays encroaching on her favorite paths. She also carried the clippers when she walked down through the Horse Field to the flowerbeds next to the vegetable garden. Every spring, Mr. Hooper planted these with the flower seeds she had ordered by catalog in February. She would do a lot of weeding in the picking-garden, before she

116

walked back up to the house, her arms and basket laden with larkspur, California poppies, mignonette, zinnias and more. She then would fill vases of all shapes and sizes with flowers, so the dining room and parlor were all aglow from mantelpiece to tea table.

One day Aunt Hat's zeal for flower arranging overpowered her, alas. All the aunts had a lifelong habit of strolling in and out of all the houses on the Sharksmouth land to see what was going on and have a friendly chat with whomever was at home. This particular day, Aunt Hat walked up to "the Cottage," where a frail elderly lady was staying. Newly released from hospital, Mrs. J. had tested her strength by teetering a few yards from the piazza to pick some flowers nearby and had just finished arranging them in a bowl on the dining room table. Aunt Hat strode into the dining room, picked up the bowl saying, "Well, I guess it's time these went out," and briskly crossing the piazza again, she threw all the flowers and water over the edge, into the woods. How Mrs. J. laughed! She was a wonderful woman and fond of the aunts in spite of their idiosyncrasies.[2]

But these instances of her quaint behavior came long after we nieces were all grown women. Back when Aunt Hat was in her twenties and early thirties her habits were not so pronounced, and her interests were wide, flexible and varied. Besides playing tournament golf and travelling in Europe, she became interested in Hampton Institute and, with Aunt Fan, began on her years-

---

[2] All the aunts had a proprietorial feeling about "the Cottage." One summer evening, during World War II, when our families were sharing the "Cottage," my sister Maly and I gave a party. Our friends all sat around on the piazza before dinner, enjoying cocktails and the sunset view of the ocean. Their voices and laughter carried all the way through the woods to the Stone House and the ears of Aunt Fan. She (a teetotaler) sneaked up the avenue and into the cottage through the kitchen door. She took the leg of lamb out of the oven and brought it into the dining room. She then opened the screen door to the piazza. "Dinner is ready," she announced firmly to the company. The next morning, when she strolled up to the Cottage again, she mildly remarked, "Well, I thought it was about time you got around to eating."

long promotion of its well-being. After the Great Chelsea Fire in
the spring of 1908, when Aunt Pedge was put in charge of
finding housing for its many victims, Aunt Hat was right there
to help her. Hat was also on hand in La Jolla, California, when
Frazier and Gladys were first setting up housekeeping. Her
presence was useful both physically and spiritually to Gladys, as
Frazier had become curiously obsessed with automobiles, and
nothing else caught his attention. She accompanied her brother
Jim on his official trip to inspect the construction of the Panama
Canal, as we already know from Bella's letter in a previous
chapter.

Probably the most interesting of all happenings in the first
decade of the 20th century was the birth of the flying machine.
Aunt Hat was as excited as the rest of America. In fact, the
whole Curtis family was air-minded, since Steen, having steadily
pursued his early ambition, was now successful and his wild
dream had become a reality. Hat was off visiting in Long Island
when she wrote of a flying meet in 1910.

> Old lady Stoddard took me to Garden City to see the flying,
> yesterday and I tell you it's awesome when Harmon has his
> paddles started and the men can hardly hold onto the machine
> with the draught and then he slides off on those silly looking
> little wheels. He circled round taking corners prettily for 10
> minutes and then had his picture taken again! Of course a lovely
> blonde rushed out to shake hands with him before he started
> amid snapping camera shutters. Mrs. Dev Emmet was there. It is
> fearfully exciting....

But the excitement was nearer to home, that year, when Hat
wrote a letter to her sister Bella, away in Venice at the time:

Monday, April 25th 1910

> A nasty damp day, just the kind of day to do a million chores
> which I don't seem to be doing, but will scratch a few lines with
> a beautiful new pen. We're terribly 'cited over Stivetts—Curtis
> and Burgess and the Flying Fish, which you know is entirely
> different from any Wright or any other, and is making a darned
> good beginning. Orders in for 7 of em at $5500 per! It seems
> mutual admiration society for Stib forks out his Cornell thesis

on why Langley's deductions were wrong and behold this feller Herring (its a Herring-Burgess Machine) pricks up his ears for *he* was Langley's assistant, and now sees Curtis was right and he & Langley wrong!! and so on, ad lib. Then Friday came Stib's big day, allowed to fly at last and he did fly real good, better than the others, *but*—by what he terms "defective control" (!!) he made a bit of an error and came dashing to ground burying the nose of the machine 4 1/2 ft. in the marsh while he took a fly over the dashboard. He covered about 300 yds. going pretty fast and beautifully till he saw the shed just ahead and then through "defective control" all right took first a shoot up to about 25 ft. & then down good and fast shattering the machine except the engine which stood like a lamb & never turned a bearing. He's perfectly thrilled—no fun like it—but we're glad he chose a soft spot. Now he's smashed it up he's ready to start for Paris! Sailing Wed. on the Majestic, I think....

The Great European War started on August 3, 1914, when Germany declared war on France and immediately sent an invading army, ruinously violating Belgium en route. While all Europe became inflamed, America remained officially neutral for two and a half years. It wasn't until February 3, 1917, that the United States broke relations with Germany, and the formal Declaration of War was pronounced on April 6, 1917. Two months later the first American troops were landing in France. But long before then, many American citizens had become concerned, and increasingly involved. When the *Lusitania* was torpedoed and sunk with great loss of American lives in 1915, feelings rose higher and higher. (Even then, however, there were people who believed that the British had secretly torpedoed the *Lusitania*, and that Britain was loudly blaming Germany for the crime in order to swing outraged America firmly onto the Allied side, and declare war on Germany. A near neighbor of the Aunts believed this, to their utter disgust.)

Soon after the invasion of Belgium and France the Aunts turned their activities to war work. Aunt Fan, though very busy with her School Committee responsibilities, managed to arrange several lectures by outstanding French and English visitors to give American audiences firsthand information of the European struggle; Aunt Hat, and a little later Aunt Bog, spent their morning hours at the center for the French wounded where, with many other Bostonians, they folded bandages and packed hospital supplies to be sent overseas. Aunt Pedge, who was a trained social worker (having graduated from the Simmons School of Social Work), went to France early in 1916, to work with the Red Cross. With headquarters in Paris, her assignment was rehabilitating refugees from the bombed-out villages of a large sector of northern France.

Finding temporary shelter, supplying food and clothing and tracking down lost family members left little time for Pedge to write letters home. But Aunt Hat wrote to her every week, and sometimes twice a week. As Pedgy, following Curtis family custom, never threw away any of these letters, they now give a lively account of life at home in Boston and Manchester during the war years. They also give, scattered here and there among the doings of family and friends, a glimpse of how civilized society in a peace-loving nation gets gradually pulled into war. Aunt Hat, as already mentioned, was a doer, not a talker, and her letters are written in very staccato fashion, her postcards more like abrupt telegrams. She managed to crowd a lot of information onto one postcard, however:

Fri Feb.18, 1916. And still no word from you in Paris. I think its only right to keep on with this line to London. You are being held up all right. Here's a letter from Mrs. Chandler asking for $1. for corsets!—Francy chases off to school com. a great deal— very booming and interesting. She is closing the engagement securing John Masefield for Mon. eve. Mar. 6th. We hear he isn't allowed to talk Dardanelles as we're keen to have him do. So we're saying "sea poems." Poor soul I hope he'll be alive. He says he's going as a private the minute he gets done here. What do you think Frazier's latest line is? "Only those for T. Roosevelt are truly anti-German"! Heavens—oh Heavens. Ma and I are reading Shakespeare these days—Two Gentlemen of Verona— real dull. Mabe was in yester. and Nell got 8 1/4 for her U. Fruit rights—the lucky dog. HSC

Quite a few of Hat's letters were opened and resealed with a sticker printed OPENED BY CENSOR. Several envelopes have envelopes with an additional sealing marked "Damaged by Seawater." During 1916, the British censors were quite active, and it appears from her remarks (though these were not censored) that the British were distinctly concerned with the shaping of American public opinion prior to 1917. "We hear James Norman Hall, the 'Kitchener's Mob' man, was given a lot of inside dope in England—but was told he couldn't let the *Atlantic Monthly* publish it," writes Hat, adding that this is because Bertrand Russell had something in the *Atlantic*, and now the British censors forbid him to speak at Harvard. "Perfectly ridiculous!", Hat comments. British censors opened her letter of December 7, 1916 but didn't object to it. After writing four pages of family news, she ends with this paragraph:

> I sent you the Nov. & Dec. *Atlantics* today. Mme. Gromitch at tea at the Sedgwicks yesterday gave Francy very interesting sidelights on the English so called Diplomacy in the Balkans. How they don't trust and play up to the Russians—Winston Churchill being the one chiefly to want to be the first to Constantinople ahead of the Russians—and all this upsettal in the Cabinet following the new Russian premier's announcement that the Allies had promised them Constantinople! She really was very enlightening on what hasn't been done out there. Today the Longfellows sent on more pamphlets sent them by Sir Gilbert Parker—perfectly enthralling, too. Accounts of Jutland send cold thrills down you.
>
> Now to hear Cesar Franck—so no more
H.S.C.

In late February 1917, before war was declared but after the United States had broken relations with Germany, Hat wrote her usual weekly account of local activities to Pedge. This letter, damaged by sea water and opened by censor, reached Paris five weeks later. While filled with anecdotes of family doings (Ma's Lunch club which the Old Lady managed nobly—Little El's seventh birthday—Bog out with Tigs, "putting herself through dog-walks as if it was an heroic duty") it tells something else. One perceives how the temperate mood in Boston was heating up:

Francy has had a time these last 3 days with M. Janvier du Theatre Antoine, sent in the hope of getting money for the Societe des Artistes Fraternelles. He gave the most moving talk with readings of pieces written during the War—a poem given to him when he visited Verdun of a poilu at the Gate of Heaven having encouragement from St. Martin and Ste. Barbara—and all of them—lovely. He charged $2. and twenty-five people came, but next time he comes, in March, we'll have him here and invite our friends. And they'll be sure to give good sums....You never knew such flying round and registering here there and everywhere as silly creatures are doing. Its impossible to make out the difference between the Special Aid cards and the Red Cross cards—and apparently all for Base Hospitals....

There is a terrible crowd calling themselves the European Peace Committee, really non-resisters—getting out reply postcards to be sent to Congressmen to say keep us out of war, and calling for a vote of the people—method and time not mentioned. John Codman is in the bunch.

Today I pitched in at packing at French wounded. A tremendous hustle and I should say 10 gentlemen packing and nailing and pasting cans & boxes. They are sending ever so much more than ever before! Such a waste of boxes from the Goodrich people who send a separate box for each hotwater bottle....Bog reads us they be taking a great pile of Victor records away from the Bernsdorf party at Halifax, fearing messages are included with them. And Ma reads an astonishing yarn of a Norwegian Capt. with his wife & a child kept for safety on the submarine that sank his boat, commanded by the gentleman who sank the Lusitania. They were toted up round Scotland & put ashore on Heligoland. And found it terribly hot when they went down & dreadfully cold when they surfaced.

And now its Sunday and we're still in an extraordinary state of almost not believing anything is going to happen. The Germans are certainly being wonderfully careful of American lives even if they did take seven Dutch boats yesterday....We didn't learn much at Ford Hall. Of course Helen was most weeping with emotion at the end holding the flag and repeating the Girls Scouts Creed!!...but even that didn't convince us there was much sense in all their excitement and Patriotism. Oh Glee. They love it. Down at French Wounded there's no such bunkum....Adair is greatly improved. Much less nervous and far less Know-it-all. He too has enrolled with 1000 odd other students in the Officers Training Corps that opened last week at Harvard and drills every afternoon from 4:30 - 5:30 except Sat & Sun. It will do him a world of good, I'm sure.

Joe [Lee] called up at 8:30 to say all aboard for Concord. It rained & melted yesterday and is 18 this morning, so it will be heavenly skating I know. The ice is thicker than ever this winter. I hope it's not our last. Six Hopkinsons are coming to dinner— Chas is still in New York. Now I'll mail this. And will start another the middle of the week. H S C

Writing on April 7th, Hat tells of the wonderful address President Wilson gave to Congress the day before, resulting in strong Congressional backing of a Declaration of War. She adds, "We're sorry for Miss Rankin, the first Congress*woman*, who hesitated & then got up & said 'I want to stand by my country, but I cannot vote for war.' She is held up as typical of Woman's foolishness."

Although spending that summer of 1917 in Manchester as usual, Aunt Hat took the commuter train to Boston regularly on Mondays and Thursdays for her work at the French Wounded. She often spent other days in town as well, for the Maverick Dispensary needed extra help ("They are doing 40 vaccinations per morning," she reports). Also, she was working in the Home Service Division of Civilian Relief, for soldiers' families. "Privates are paid $30 per month, & are expected to give $20 of it to their families. A $10. Honorarium extra for those who volunteered. But the Draft takes family men with 2 children," she tells Pedgy.

By autumn that year, every letter Hat wrote told of a male friend or cousin sailing for war and of others returning badly wounded, with tales of ships rammed by savage submarines. In November, after the Boston Symphony Orchestra had begun its season of weekly concerts, she wrote in outrage that the Orchestra was forced to play the "Star Spangled Banner" at the beginning of every concert. It was an insult to the audience, the musicians and Karl Muck, the Orchestra's superbly talented conductor. She was also disgusted at the ridiculous talk going round that Muck was a German sympathizer.

Throughout Aunt Hat's wartime letters, casual comments about the Boston Symphony Orchestra and its distinguished conductor appear again and again. Reading them seventy years later, they seem like the refrain of a mournful ballad telling how easily the best creations of civilized man are desecrated, trampled under the heavy foot of War. In 1916 Hat wrote Pedge about a recent evening, driving out to Cambridge with "the Higs" (Henry L. Higginson, founder of the Boston Symphony Orchestra, and his wife) to a concert at Sanders Theatre. On the way, "Uncle Henry" remarked, "This may be one of the last concerts the Orchestra will ever give." On being asked why, he said he didn't think the Boston Symphony Orchestra could survive the War if America entered it. In 1917, after the United States broke relations with Germany, Hat's weekly letters often tell of the beautiful Brahms or Beethoven she enjoyed at Symphony Hall last Friday afternoon. But as the concert season progresses, so does Hat's indignation about those idiotic Bostonians (now increasing in number) who are forever dragging Muck's Teutonic origin into any conversation about the Orchestra's magnificent performance.

The climax came in the spring of 1918. In Paris, Pedge had the first news of it from her mother:

Boston, March 29, 1918

Dear little Peggi,

It is Good Friday and sister Hat is busy getting King's Chapel ready for the fray....Boston is all wrought up about the arrest of Muck just the day before the great day of his life, the performance of the Bach Passion Music, which he has never given before. They call him an Enemy Alien but I don't know that makes him one.

Well anyhow, he is put in prison for the time being....It began with people in Providence wanting the Star Spangled Banner on their concert and they announce that Muck had refused to play it. So Mr. Higginson hurried to print that M. did not know that he had been asked for it, Mr. H. & Mr. Ellis had suppressed the fact—but anyway, M. had never refused and now has played it at every concert since—where it is quite incongruous. But no, he is a dangerous enemy. The Passion Music was given with a substitute conducting as well as he could....

In the same envelope with her mother's was a letter from Hat:

...Francy and Mark Howe have been circulating a backing-up support of H.L.Hig and his concerts, very well expressed—but today they are changing the wording a bit as *Muck was arrested Monday eve* as an alien enemy, but what or how much they have on him nobody knows yet, and some of us feel quite doubtful yet as to whether the arrest was necessary....I'd like very much to know what they've got on him. He is so conspicuous and obvious that you'd think they'd use a lesser light of the Orchestra if any.

But two days later Hat was writing:

...It is strange about Muck. It now transpires he is arrested under the White Slave Act, writing rotten letters to the Young Girl—sister of the one who plays golf around here. She's always been extremely conspicuous sitting in the front row at the Concerts. It seems as if she had kept his letters and now has turned against him and handed them over to the Dept. of Justice —rather awkward of her, I should think. She's a poor sort, evidently....

A full month went by before Hat mentioned Karl Muck again, near the end of a long letter filled with other topics:

April 30, 1918

...That's quite a hustle you've all done with your bedding and food for the hordes of poor refugees, isn't it? If we can't yet do much on the Front, its fine to have us do good things in the rear. We haven't made out where they are being sent—how far South. We do get more and more word of the big numbers of soldiers, even if still perfectly green that have gone overseas—and the quietness of their going, its secretness is thrilling. We heard t'other night of 17 train loads of sojers embarking on five transports all done after dark and before daylight from East Boston—the steamers coming in and out in the dark; 87,000 in a month from N.Y. and so on. I take it you are by way of hearing a good bit of whats doing—which we no longer get.

Gutzon Borglum, the sculptor, is figuring large at the mome, as he is supposed to have been directed by the President to find out what the matter was with the aeroplane building. "We" think he's a crook and the Senators seem to think so too. And speaking of crooks it now reaches us Muck has been a masterhand —but our people knew it and were gathering tidbits from him. Whether tis so, and Mr. Hig either knew it, or was purposely kept in the dark we know not. Anyway, he was taken in for sending obscene letters in the mail, and offered a choice of Court proceedings on White Slave Act, or internment—both being under Federal jurisdiction. He is said to have been very much surprised his letters were thought so evil, as he said nobody would think anything of that in Europe i.e. Germany, I guess. Do you hear of Germany calling for more children and of officers being given stated districts with names of available & suitable ladies? Ellen Em has a letter of a spinster reporting herself as being "Officially pregnant." Wonderful morals—and system. Oh yes. The Permanent Charity Fund have voted $1000 to the Maverick!! We'll get a new worker for the office quick.

H S C

Before leaving Aunt Hat's war-time correspondence, one more letter should be included, for it shows an American attitude toward Soviet Russia quite different from that of "the Cold War" prevailing so many years. This letter was written in April 1919—nearly six months after Armistice Day.

...We had a wonderful time yesterday listening spellbound to Raymond Robbins for two and a half hours, who is certainly an orator, telling us of what he did and said and saw in Russia from July 1917 to June 1918, and it seemed as if he and Col. Thompson, the Head of the Red Cross Commission, guessed right all along as to the march of events—being of course for Kerensky till they saw his day was over, very soon believing in the Soviet Government system, chasing right over to Trotsky and frankly telling him they'd been dead against him, but seeing he had the power came to him to sanction their work. Always Robbins seemed to get at the true (or truer) state of facts than the Embassy and after he (Robbins) got a pretty good secret service going and there was a difference in the reports between his service and the French and British ones, *his* were taken to be truer and sent to Paris and London and when Thompson felt he had to get to Washington to state his beliefs and stop the misinformation he stopped in London and talked two hours to Lloyd George who was so impressed with this other side of the story that he sent Bruce-Lockheart p.d.q. and in no time Lockheart and Robbins and Thompson were in perfect agreement. And yet never did the Entente get round to taking action, and in consequence failed to rescue all those guns and ammunition from falling into the Germans hands and failed to stop the export of copper and aluminum and other raw materials from going to Germany via Sweden and Finland—all of which stoppage Trotsky was ready to do. Robbins says that never once did either Lenin or Trotsky fail to keep their word with himand they had the power sure enough. He firmly declares he is dead against the Bolsheviki because they are undemocratic and unmoral in their methods—but he distinguished between them and the Soviet system, which is government after our Town Meeting style.

Nuff sed now. H S C

When World War I finally ended, Aunt Hat in no wise slackened her pace. She could now spend more hours helping out at the Maverick Dispensary and turn once again to promoting the well-being of Hampton Institute. She also had added responsibilities, for she had been made a Director of the Associated Charities during the War. The Associated Charities had always been Pedgy's field of concern before she went to France. Though younger than Hat, Pedge had been the dominating one of this pair of sisters ever since they were "the Little Girls" at the end of the long line of Curtis siblings. It is typical of Aunt Hat's modesty that in one of her war-time letters she remarks "John Moors says that at the Ass. Char. Mtg. yesterday they said all sorts of praiseworthy things of me! That since Miss Margaret had gone Miss Harriot had done fine. I wonder what they mean?" And when she was made a Director of the Association, she wrote Pedge it was "an honor I could do without."

In the spring of 1923, my grandmother died. Her lungs had been gradually failing, and during her last two or three years she was wracked with wheezing and an incurable cough. (Laughing merrily—but affectionately—Aunts Bog and Pedge told how after a particularly bad coughing spell, their mother had murmured, "Do I *have* to go on living?" and Aunt Fan had replied, "Of course not, Ducky!" in her typical brisk but helpful way.) After their mother's death, the Aunts continued to live in both the Boston and Manchester houses, as always. Aunt Fan continued in her role as family arbitrator and household manager, though as years rolled on, she gradually, and gracefully, ceded her domain to Aunt Pedge. Gracefully, I say, because Aunt Fan always looked for peaceful solutions, smilingly arrived at. Aunt Hat was far too wise to interfere in matters of household management, though she would quite often tell Francey it was "time we had lobster again," or "*Don't* let Sarah overcook the roast beef *this* time," for she was always interested in food. She was particularly enthusiastic about fruits; in the blueberry season she loved to corral a niece or two to accompany her on an expedition to Dogtown Common, a wild and grassy upland beyond Gloucester, where we spent the morning stripping the blueberry bushes growing among the cellar-holes and pastures of a deserted village.

A busy and most rewarding season for Aunt Hat came at the end of summer, when the apples, pears and quinces were beginning to ripen in the old horse field, below the tennis court at Manchester. Before they were ready to eat, she carried basketsful of pears (Seckels and Beurry Boscs) up to the house, and deposited them in the chest-on-chest in the dining room. Here, in its dark drawers, they ripened slowly and perfectly. The great mahogany chest-on-chest was at least seven feet high, and was crowned by a little statue of Minerva, exquisitely carved, standing between two curving mahogany scrolls. It was made by MacIntyre, master-craftsman of Salem. When the Museum of Fine Arts in Boston acquired this early American masterpiece later, the curators were horrified to learn that the Aunts used it for garden produce. Of course the Aunts did! We nieces weren't at all surprised. As for the quinces, Aunt Hat let them ripen on the trees before tackling them. Raw quinces are inedible even when they are ripe, for their flesh is almost impenetrable. Aunt Hat spent hours preparing them for cooking, sitting out in the sun on the piazza whittling away at their cork-like substance, quartering and coring them and stopping now and then to sniff their wonderful smell. The thought of delicious quince sauce and marmalade spurred her on, and she kept a spare paring-knife handy in case a niece might stop by and help for a few minutes.

But there were four seasons of autumn harvesting she had to miss, because she was away at Hampton Institute, "pinch-hitting" as a dean. Over the years that she had helped Hampton, she had come to know its governors and management—and they to know her. In 1927, President Gregg called on her for help. She quickly wrote to Pedge, who was off golfing in the Southwest:

> ...and now I come to the most dreadful proposal that seems utterly incredible. A week ago Gregg wired could he see me today—No idea what for. Well, he thinks he wants me to come for a year anyhow as Dean of Women—i.e. Girls. Can you beat it? I think he's crazy. Its simply preposterous even if flattering. I don't see it at first glance certainly, but I agreed to talk it over with Gertrude Peab. and her pa. It seems to me dreadfully alarming. I gather he needs a stopgap until a crackajack finishes Cornell. Its from next Sept. 1st. Of course I'm overcome to be thought possible—but certainly don't feel in the least capable. Gregg says don't judge about yourself as to suitability if others believe you are all right. He felt himself totally unprepared to head Hampton.
>
> It would be interesting no doubt—even if not what I call my line. Would you screw yourself up to it if you were me? Isn't it extraordinary? Most upsetting. *Speak up*. Oh Whee.

Ten days later, she was writing again to Pedgy, who had finished her golfing and moved on.

> *Sat. Mar 19th. and you at my canyon*
> Lobster again—Why couldn't you wire when you knew when

you were leaving. I've sent important letters to N.B. where I trust you'll get some day. Have you got wind of the Hampton proposition? That I'm to be queen of the May—me. Dean of Women. ooooooh. I'm reading about it for dear life and Gregg wants me to go all over the lot to discuss it and learn from Tennessee to Penn School....I can't see any good reason why I shouldn't take a shot at it—and know it would be good for me to do so. But ain't it awful....

Overcoming her qualms and modesty, she went to Hampton in September 1927 and stayed there as Dean of Women for the next four years, only interrupted by brief vacations at home. The world of Hampton Institute was very different from the world of Boston and Manchester. Founded in 1868 as a school for emancipated slaves, it had grown to the top-rank of Negro colleges and was a large, busy community of black Americans. Their heritage was very different from that of a New Englander steeped in the Anglo-Saxon traditions of Old Bostonian families— she must have felt lonely at the end of a hard day's work. Several years after she had completed her Deanship, I once tried to start her talking about her Hampton experiences. She only said, "Well, I got them to keep the lights on in the auditorium while movies were going on." How typical of Aunt Hat! Of course she wouldn't expand on her own triumphs and tribulations, the hard work and her isolation from familiar surroundings.

It was Hampton Institute, however, that started her off on what was probably the most rewarding venture of her life. While attending church on Sundays and listening to the Hampton Choir, she became aware of one particular voice, outstanding in its clarity and beauty. This was the voice of a young girl named Dorothy Maynor. As a music lover and avid concert- and opera-goer, Aunt Hat had heard most of the great singers of her time. She recognized that Dorothy's voice was extremely rare. This beauty must be given to the world, she decided—if Dorothy had the fortitude to go through with the necessary musical training. Dorothy had. With the steady friendship and complete financial backing of Aunt Hat, this unknown little black girl from the South rose to the top of the artistic world. It took time and hard work. Dorothy studied with masters of voice-training both here and abroad; in New York Klamroth was her teacher, in Berlin she not only learnt the language, but became expert in rendering German lieder. Familiarizing herself with opera, she practiced arias until she could sing them with consummate artistry.

Finally, the great moment came. In the summer of 1939, when the Boston Symphony Orchestra was in the Berkshires for its annual summer festival, Dorothy sang for Koussevitsky, in a private audition. The world-famous orchestra conductor was astonished and greatly moved. The next day, he introduced her as a "New Kirsten Flagstad" to the complete orchestra, assembled in the big music shed. After she sang for them, the musicians enthusiastically agreed with their director. Koussevitsky then told her she would very soon sing in Symphony Hall, in the regular series of Boston Symphony Orchestra concerts.

The news media immediately took up the story of Dorothy: the *Boston Globe's* headline was "NATIVE FLAGSTAD BELIEVED FOUND" and went on to describe the program she sang in the music shed of arias sung by dramatic- and mezzo-sopranos and coloraturas and how "the famous conductor was heard to comment about Miss Maynor's varied style, clarity of voice and wonderful musicality." The *Herald's* headline was "KOUSSEVITSKY HAILS SOPRANO. Says Negress New Kirsten Flagstad." The *New York Times* gave a whole column on page 14 to Dorothy, describing how she had mastered the most difficult songs, praising her rendition of "Sleep, why dost thou leave me," and went on to say that "All those conversant with the vocal art agree that a new songstress of startling powers has been discovered." Though the *Boston Evening Transcript* had been rather snooty in its report of that concert in the Festival music shed, saying "there was no need for a high lyric soprano to venture into Wagner," the *New York Times* said, "...she followed with an extraordinarily sure and electrifying account of the 'Ho - Yo - To - Ho' from Die Walkurie."

Aunt Hat was ecstatic. She immediately wrote to Pedgy (in Europe again): "I *do* do such dumb things, as thou knowest—

but there's one thing I've made no mistake about, and that's Dorothy." She went on, amid showers of exclamation marks and an occasional "Whee!" to quote from the newspapers and said, "The Fairy Story of Dorothy Maynor was given over WAAB, and I wondered ahead of time how awful it might be. But it wasn't bad. I was not quite the Fairy Godmother—but merely a lover of Music....Isn't it all thrilling? Exactly the kind of publicity we want. Couldn't be better. Too good to be true." Indeed, with this acclaim, Dorothy was well launched on a promising career. Over the next few years she was in considerable demand, and delighted audiences on a wide circuit of exquisite concert performances. But Aunt Hat's dream of a life-long career for her was not to be realized. One day when I stopped by the Aunts' house, I found Aunt Hat sitting alone, a grim expression on her face and an opened letter on her lap. "There!", she barked, pointing to the letter. "I knew it! She's going to take care of a darn fool man and will never sing again."

Of course Aunt Hat would never impose her wishes on another human being, glorious though her dream had been, and generous her motive. I recently came across a note written in pencil, presumably the draft of what she had written after receiving Dorothy's letter:

April 4, 1942

My dear D. Indeed I rejoice with you in your new found happiness and feel glad to have you properly excited as a person truly in love should be. It was because you seemed so calm and collected that I wondered if the right emotions had touched you. Now you feel differently—and so do I.

This beautiful experience will enhance your powers of expression—and if your attention is not too much divided your work will not suffer.

Don't worry about my disapproving. I am very happy that you are happy. For I know you have been lonely and it is time for companionship. May you find in Mr. Rooks the sympathy and understanding and enjoyment of the beauties you so much feel — that sharing your enthusiasms with him will give you lasting joy.

Now you feel sure of yourself, I say Bless you, my very dear Friend.

Dorothy did not give up singing entirely after she married the Reverend Shelby Rooks. In fact, when President Eisenhower took office and his Inaugural Ceremony was broadcast nationwide, it was Dorothy Maynor's voice singing "America the Beautiful" that soared across the country from sea to shining sea. But after settling in Harlem, where her husband had his parish, she soon became engrossed in a new project. There were many schoolchildren and teenagers in the neighborhood with nothing to do after school hours but drift about in the streets. Seeing there was no opportunity for employment and no stimulus for individual ambition or self-fulfillment, Dorothy thought she could help. She began by setting up afternoon classes in music, painting and dance, in whatever space was available in nearby buildings. Later, she turned to Wall Street, and bearding several millionaire lions in their dens, she collected enough money to build a complete new facility, with ample space for classes, rooms for private lessons and an auditorium. Today, the Harlem School of the Arts, conceived and founded by Dorothy Maynor, holds an important and greatly valued place among New York's cultural assets.

Dorothy directed the school for some years, constantly working on ways to improve it. And often she and Shelby Rooks came for summer vacations at Manchester, for of course Aunt Hat remained a lifelong friend. This friendship was deeply treasured by Dorothy, who never forgot who had given her a start on life. Eventually, when Aunt Hat began to show signs of old age in her late eighties, Dorothy often called me from New York, asking "How's my friend? Remember, I'll drop everything, anytime if you think I can give her any help."

Aunt Hat, who had never been much of a conversationalist, used fewer and fewer words as she grew older. Her keen observations and strong opinions were expressed in a vehement shorthand of verbal barks, and her loving concern shone through abrupt sentences. One day, one of her unmarried great nieces was picking beans in the vegetable garden when Aunt Hat approached her and asked, "Do you go to any parties?" The niece said "Yes," and Aunt Hat stumped away to the strawberry bed. But she was soon back to say, "If you're going to be a spinster, I want you to know it's a very good life. You have all of the children, but none of the bother." Then she stumped away again.

Her loving concern was bewilderingly disguised when she telephoned me early one morning. She used to telephone many mornings in those years after the last of her sisters had died, and she lived on, alone. But this morning, she called me before I was fully awake. "Ibb, we don't want twins, do we," was her opening remark, half question, half statement. It took me a few seconds to realize what was on her mind: her great-niece Lola had just given birth prematurely to twins so fragile that they were now under very special care at the hospital. Aunt Hat had probably lain awake half the night worrying about them and dear Lola. "Of *course* we want twins!" I answered. "Lots of people have twins—there's nothing bad about twins! They grow up just as well as any other babies. Everybody loves twins!" A visit to the hospital's preemie ward, a day or two later, gave her added peace of mind, for the little ones were gaining well. She saw the twins often after that, for Lola and Don Minifie always brought them along when they came to see Aunt Hat. At her ninetieth birthday party the twins were present, each in a carrying basket, set on a table. Three years later, when it was explained to them that Aunt Hat had died, little Polly exclaimed, "I'm so glad we knew her when she was young!"

Certainly young in spirit, Aunt Hat lived out her last years. In old age she maintained her enthusiasms as freshly as she had in her early fifties, before she had undergone a serious colostomy operation. After that, she had never allowed her spirit to be hampered by the apparatus she was forced to wear. When wintering in Boston, she still went to Symphony concerts by subway, all through her eighties, and walked downtown across the Common to go shopping. She bought herself a sprightly blue silk dress when she was eighty-seven. She gaily welcomed friends, old and new, and loved playing cards, laughing merrily whether she won or lost at "Oh Hell" (a version of "Black Mary"). She kept up her interest and support in good causes, both local and world-wide. When living in Manchester, she took brisk walks, loved picking raspberries and flowers, exclaimed joyously over a bright blue sky or a perfectly delicious lobster. One of her favorite occupations was hunting for mushrooms on the golf links, though she no longer played the game.

Her interest in the world around her remained as strong as ever. When a great niece introduced a friend from Kenya, Aunt Hat may have been momentarily startled by his height, blackness, and African robes. "Good for you, young man! Good for you!" she exclaimed and warmly pumped his hand. A year or two later, her international outlook shone forth again: she was by now ninety-two and physically weaker, but still wanting to walk half a mile down the Lane (Ocean Street) to see the waves breaking in a long curve along White Beach. Mary and Ellen, two faithful retainers, went with her. They were on their way back when I and a visiting foreigner met them in the Lane. The walk had really been too much for Aunt Hat; she was bowed over, shuffling slowly with bent knees, clutching the elbows of Mary and Ellen on either side. "Hello, Aunt Hat! This is Mr. Hemblin from Australia," said I. Aunt Hat raised her head slightly and crowed out, "Three cheers for Australia!" and shuffled on.

I was with Aunt Hat much of the time, those last years. Though she never complained, it was plain she needed someone to talk to. I was the handiest of her nieces, for the others were busy with their families elsewhere. Her physical needs were tended to by devoted Mary, and by Katherine, a retired practical nurse who would take no money for the gently efficient care she provided, because she felt it a privilege to take care of this endearing patient. Aunt Hat and I spent many evenings together at Manchester in the big stone house where she was born. We each had our favorite sofa, facing each other across the hearth of the living room. We would both be reading, I with my spectacles on, she with none. She had never worn glasses and didn't need them now. Aunt Hat had taken up serious reading very lately, for, she explained, Pedgy and she had been so busy playing golf that they had missed all the good books, and it was time she got going on them. She was in the midst of *Lorna Doone* that last year, but it was slow going, for she kept interrupting herself (and me) with irrelevant thoughts that burst out in brief comments and questions. These were almost always about up-to-the-minute happenings, for she was not one to indulge herself in nostalgia.

Many of her nieces and nephews were on hand to celebrate Aunt Hat's ninety-third birthday on June 30th, 1974, and she was as sprightly as ever with abrupt remarks to cover her delight and affection. But as the summer months passed on into autumn, her legs could no longer keep up with her spirited impulses.

There were no more brisk walks along the shore to revel in the rhythm of the nearby shining sea, and no trips to the vegetable garden. Even on beautiful sunny days, with all the zeal she could muster, she found it difficult to walk any further than to a comfortable chair outdoors on the piazza. Of course she didn't ever complain, but she *did* remark one day, "Well, I don't think that year of being ninety-two was as much fun as ninety-one." The moon was full October 15th, that year. Mary came into the parlor in the evening to announce, "There's a full moon tonight, Miss Harriot. Don't you want to go out and see it?" "You bet! Help me up," said Aunt Hat. We got her up off her sofa and walked her outdoors. We all three stood silent, our faces upturned to the enormous mystery above us, the brightly shining sphere and the glittering canopy of stars, each faithful to its eternal orbit. Aunt Hat finally said, in a lower voice than usual, "I wonder why they're there." Then she wanted to go indoors. She died ten days later.

Aunt Pedge, c. 1900

Chapter Seven

Aunt Pedge
Margaret Curtis 1883-1965

The youngest of the Aunts, Aunt Pedge was also the youngest of the ten Curtis children. When one thinks of all those lively games the children's parents encouraged, one can easily see why the youngest of them, when fully grown, was competitive, authoritative, and needing acclaim. She was also infinitely goodhearted and well-intentioned, a great athlete, a professional social worker, an able administrator, a good carpenter and auto-mechanic. She loved working outdoors at Manchester. While the other aunts strolled through the woods hunting for gypsy moth nests and walking the dogs, Aunt Pedge was likely to be down on the shore path, crowbar in hand, earnestly prying a boulder out of the way. The rock might be a fifty-pounder or a three-hundred pounder, but she would keep at it, and succeed, no matter how long it took to finish the Herculean task. Probably she would have an axe nearby, as well, to tackle a scrub-oak tree that was interfering with the growth of a struggling pine. The aunts all preferred pine trees.

A photograph of little Peggy at age three shows her in a fluffy dress cuddling a doll. In all later childhood pictures, she is wearing britches, like her brothers Harry, Frazier and Jim. She started early to emulate them and continued to do so throughout her life. She never showed any femininity toward men, and no man ever fell in love with her, as far as I know, though many admired her accomplishments. One cannot help but wonder whether she was born to love women instead of men, or whether that boisterous and competitive family environment overwhelmed any budding femininity innate within her. But what did it matter? Aunt Pedge led a very full life; she was outstanding in her professional work and a champion in sports. She vigorously alternated these two occupations during more than six decades.

Her zeal for sports began as soon as she was able to toss a ball and swing a stick. She was already interested in golf; when a stocky little ten-year-old, she wrote the following letter to her big brother Steen:

> Dear Stib,
>
> Will you get for me all the stamps you can as I am trying to get all I can....I am on a baseball nine which is lots of fun. I am pitch and short. Jim did play golf, but as they—Mr. Camel—gave him 3 for a handicap, which is next to scratch and the person he was playing with had 14 and best besides, Jib had no Show for it. I have been riding the big blue bike quite a lot and it is great fun. You must answer this note right off and don't forget the stamps. Get them clean if you can. That is all I can think of for now, so good by from
>> Margaret
>
> Oh yes, in the athletics, *Yale* won 60 to 40. Very poor.

Letters written twelve years later from camp illustrate again Peg's full-bodied enthusiasm for sports. Putnam Camp, in the Adirondacks, was the scene of many budding romances during annual houseparties for eligible young Bostonians of both sexes, but Peggy's letters are full of nothing but baseball, tennis, running races and boat races. Even hiking has become a kind of race:

> Yesterday practically the whole crowd did Giant (Mountain), and would you believe it. Yours truly and Evelyn arrived side by side the first to the top! Without having stopped but once on the level. I didn't lose my breath once nor feel tired anywhere, but that's what minus 15 pounds does for one. It was GREAT!

As a teenager at Miss Winsor's School, Peggy Curtis had a number of good friends, and often one of these classmates turned to her for advice, for she exuded a sense of strength and sympathy. Her best friend at school was Rachel Brooks, a very pretty girl with many attentive boy-friends. Dozens of her letters to Peg remain, describing them glowingly—and how nerve-wracking it was when Dick came to call, but Larry suddenly appeared that same evening; how embarrassing it was to be sitting with George on a bench in the Public Gardens when Mrs. Q., that friend of her mother's, walked by. A year or two later, Peg acted as a go-between when her cousin, Sumner Appleton, fell madly in love with Rachel, wanting Peg to arrange a succession of rendezvous for him where his meetings with Rachel would look like chance encounters. Peg was obviously a valuable confidante for each of them, for so many letters were written to her by both. And letters from other close friends, past school-mates, also abound. One says, "You have a sort of protecting way with you that makes me feel quite clinging and small," and a few years later another friend writes, "You were the person I wanted to be more like especially again and again. Also longed to be more like you so that I could accomplish more....one night I spent hours cursing myself that I was too stupid and unlike a grand girl I knew." A letter from a girl who was a siren among men states she "behaved rather naughtily with 'Ben' and also 'Mr. Parker.' Oh Peg, why aren't I like you, doing *good* things?"

After graduating from the Winsor School, Peg enrolled in the School of Social Work at Simmons College. Social work had only recently become established as a profession, and Peg was in this school's first graduating class, in 1904. The next year she began working for the Associated Charities of Boston (later named the Family Welfare Society), with which her sisters Fan and Hat were already involved. Serving first as an East Boston "visitor," she was soon appointed to committees, and by 1910 to the Board of Directors. In the Great Chelsea Fire of 1908, she held a significant role in organizing care and shelter for the hundreds of families driven from their homes. During her work as a Family Welfare visitor in East Boston, she had become aware of the inadequacy of medical facilities there. In 1909, she and her sister Hat established the Maverick Dispensary, an out-patient clinic, in that densely populated community of mostly Italian families. Starting out with one doctor and one dentist, the Dispensary served 2000 patients that first year. By the mid 1930s, 40,000 patients' visits were being recorded annually, and the staff included three dentists, an eye specialist, a "nerve" specialist, and two to three internists. Patients were charged twenty cents for eye and dental service. Otherwise, doctor's fees and medicines were covered by private donations, mostly acquired by the Curtis sisters through an annual appeal letter. Now, however, the Maverick Dispensary no longer exists, its services having been taken over by improved health facilities in East Boston.

All the while Margaret Curtis was doing her charitable work, she was also pursuing her career in sports. As mentioned earlier, she had qualified as a contestant in the Women's National Golf Championship as a child of thirteen, and she went right on from there, entering tournaments up and down the Atlantic seaboard, and in England, Scotland and Ireland. From every tee, her powerful drive astonished onlookers, including the sports press, for her drive was stronger and longer than any other woman's. Her putting, however, was erratic; but eventually, with her competitive zeal ever spurring her on, she learned to wield her putter with more subtle accuracy.

The game of golf got under way in America in the early 1890s and the first national women's tournament was held in 1895, the year before little pig-tailed Peggy qualified. Playing constantly with her brothers and sisters on their own home course, the Essex County Club in Manchester, she and Hatty (and their brother Jim as well) were soon serious contenders in tournaments farther afield, and accounts of the Curtis Sisters' prowess appeared more and more often in the press. There are still two fat scrapbooks at Manchester, filled with newspaper accounts of their matches, play by play, and dramatic photographs of the girls in full swing; dressed in shirtwaists with high, boned collars, and heavy skirts swishing the ground, they are smiling under extraordinary flat hats pinned to their high-piled hair. In 1901, the *Manchester Cricket* reported, "Miss M.C. again demonstrated her remarkable ability as a golf player, winning the cup of Women's golf Thursday, defeating Grace Keyes the former champion...." Peg won the State Championship three times after that, in 1907, 1908 and 1914. Between 1900 and 1905, she and Hatty both entered—and placed—in the National Championships, though Peg's putting was still unsatisfactory.

Margaret Curtis, age 13, qualifies and plays in the Women's National Golf Championship, 1896.

While Hat and Peg were off competing in the Nationals, their loyal followers at home were, of course, earnestly encouraging them with letters. "Well, children, we are as usual watching your work with long distance spy-glasses," wrote Mrs. Curtis in 1905, and a few days later, tense with excitement, she exhorted Hatty: "Tell Peg for Heaven's sake to *putt* the ball and hole the putts in the finals!" Sister Bella was equally pressing: "As you say, the games thus far are going well! But why an 86, say your grasping sisters—the *Transcript* says 'Wiseacres might pick Miss Margaret Curtis for the winner, but she has failed at the critical moment too often.'"

In spite of enthusiastic goading from the home front, neither of the Curtis sisters triumphed until 1906, when the woman golf Champion of America was Harriot S. Curtis. The following year Margaret Curtis won the Women's National Golf Championship, beating her sister Hatty in the final match. "The sisters

143

played golf for all it was worth," said the *Transcript*, "and the match was the most exciting of the tournament." Near the end, Peg wowed the spectators with a 220 yard drive. After this victory in 1907, Peg won the National Championship twice more. In 1911, she defeated an Englishwoman whom all the papers declared "unbeatable." Peg must have been practicing her short strokes on the green assiduously, for it was reported, "Through mastery over Mrs. Hurd in her own stronghold, accurate approaching and good putting, the Boston girl gave the Briton her first championship defeat this side of the Atlantic." Peg won the National Championship again, the next year, in spite of a bandaged hand which she had cut on a broken window just before the match. Three times National Golf Champion and one time National Tennis Champion (with Evelyn Sears, winning the Women's Doubles in 1908), Peg continued tournament playing for several more decades.

Her competitive spirit was still rampant fifty-five years after her first national triumph. "Aunt Hat," I said, sitting down to lunch with my then very elderly aunts, "I never knew you won the National Championship before Aunt Pedge did...." Before Aunt Hat could open her mouth, Aunt Pedge proclaimed, "She never would have if I hadn't had my appendix out that year."

Though thirst for recognition and hunger for supremacy were elemental to her golfing victories, they were insignificant in her professional work. In this, her genuine kindliness and urge to help her fellow-beings came to the fore, coupled with sound judgment and a capacity for hard work. She strove as faithfully in her professional commitments as she did at perfecting her golf strokes, those early years after graduating from the Simmons School. Her mother, in a flippant post-card to "Isab," remarks, "Peggy goes faithfully to Boston every day and gets epileptic wives committed to Brighton or somewhere after chasing husband over wharves and ships to secure his signature." Even during those triumphant championship years, when the name Margaret Curtis was writ large on every newspaper's sports page, she held to her professional duties. In a 1910 postcard from Manchester, her mother says, "Pedge defeated someone, then went to

Boston for a meeting, and expects to play mixed doubles this p.m." It was not until several years later that Aunt Pedge's most serious and effective work began.

In February of 1916, she sailed to Paris to join Mrs. Shurtleff, the head of the Student Atelier Association, an affiliate of the Red Cross. There volunteers worked to feed, clothe and later to house the many refugees that streamed from the war zone into the city, starving, ill and frequently in need of medical attention. Some volunteers worked in the 'Vestière,' where donated clothing was stored. Here they outfitted whole families, cutting and reshaping large garments when necessary for the many ragged children. Other volunteers were assigned as "Visitors," to attend to the needs of families that had been allotted temporary shelter in the city. "It was my duty to train and direct the visitors and make calls," Peg wrote later. "We were there as a group of complete strangers, totally ignorant of the resources of Paris, and of the different charitable organizations interested in refugees."

Understandably, the French agencies were skeptical of these newly arrived American volunteers, many of whom had no working knowledge of the French language. Peggy Curtis was immediately aware of the need to win the trust and cooperation of these agencies. She took French lessons twice a week and started planning for good coordination of the activities practiced by the various agencies, local, European and American, working with civilian war-victims. It was not until after the United States entered the war, and the American Red Cross took a prominent role in this work that her proposal for coordination was put into practice, with due recognition of her foresight.

Meanwhile, that first year she was in Paris, she worked hard to learn the methods prescribed by her boss, Mrs. Shurtleff. For someone accustomed to directing charitable operations in Boston, it must have been difficult now to be accepting directions, but Peg did so, with graceful humility. One of her first tasks was to make out a format for information cards, each to serve as a case record of an individual client or family. After much thought, she wrote home:

145

I took my face card up to Mrs. Shurtleff this morning. She rather laughed at its elaborateness, but said if I wanted it, and as I had agreed to stand all expenses and leave it so that anyone else could use the system, I was welcome to go ahead....I am trying hard to go slowly and keep from forming opinions too soon. I like Mrs. Shurtleff very much and I think her judgment seems very good...naturally, I don't even know that much....

Soon after she arrived in Paris, Peg began thinking about acquiring an automobile. It would help with the Atelier's operations enormously, in expediting the visitors' field work and for transporting goods. But how could one get a car? In 1916, before America had entered the war, no cars were available for civilians. Mrs. Shurtleff and the others were at first doubtful, and gave Peg no encouragement. Furthermore, even if she could track down a car, how was an American woman, not very fluent in French, going to persuade authorities to grant her a driving license—in a country where men only were car-drivers, chauffeurs, and mechanics? The idea was inconceivable, beyond anyone's faculty of imagination. Peg reached so many dead ends in her car hunt that she wired home to see if the Curtis car could be sent over. In the end, however, she was able to buy one, once she had been given permission to take a driving test and had passed it. "Mrs. Shurtleff let out such a screech of joy when she found we had got one that she made everyone run to her assistance," Peg wrote her family.

Wherever she and her car went, they caused a stir, Peg wrote to Hatty:

We were charmed by a group of 17 year old boys this afternoon, who, as we came along in Fordy, clapped their hands and shouted "C'est chic, ça!" It is ludicrous how amazed they are at seeing a woman drive. You hear murmurs of "C'est une femme qui conduise elle-meme" and such like.

Even the French army reacted: "Vivent les Fords!" cried a group of smiling poilus, saluting as Peg chugged past them.

As the work at the Americans' Atelier increased, there was less and less time for letter-writing. At home, the Curtis family sent off letter after letter, urging Pedge to write—even if only a postcard—so they would have some idea of how things were going and what she was up to. Every two or three weeks, she would respond.

Our days glide from us like nothing at all. Eleanor Parker is in charge of unpacking and listing the cases which come, which takes a varying amount of time each week, as we never know what's coming. But most of our time is really spent in investigating and visiting the new families which come in at the rate of about three a day. We try to draw the line at "Paris poor" but where there's a problem of sickness or acute misery *due to war*, we do plunge a bit. Alice (Sturgis) has taken over the ouvrier, which means quite a lot of work. One morning a week she gives out work and pays for what they bring in; but besides that she has to see to having things cut out and decide what's best to be made out of the quaint things that are sent, such as little boys' pants out of a lady's riding habit skirt....

The Vestière is open every Wednesday and Saturday morning, and they usually fit out three or four families each time, meaning 20 to 30 souls with pretty complete clothes. The women in that department are very expert by now, and make a sales-woman at Jordan Marsh look like a beginner—one thrusting a kid into a pair of pants while another is putting on boots.

...I'm the boss of the outside work and it's beginning to go a little better, although our commonest problem is T.B. and the sanitorium possibilities almost nil, it's hard to accomplish much.

Actually, she must have accomplished a great deal, because Mrs. Shurtleff was aghast when she heard Pedgy's plan to go home in June for the summer. "She would give her eye teeth to have me stay on," wrote Pedge. After much to-ing and fro-ing of transAtlantic letters, she did go home in July for two months of family life in Manchester—but sailed again for France in September, in response to a letter from Mrs. Shurtleff demanding her return in no uncertain terms.

This time, Peg brought with her her dear friend and long-time companion Mabel Sturgis, and immediately they were both immersed in work—which had become more and more pressing during Peg's absence. She found time, however, to write the following description of Paris:

> The streets are, as you know, extraordinarily dark, both for the benefit of the Zepps, and for an economy of coal. For the same reason, all stores except those lit by candles, have been ordered closed at 6 instead of 7. It makes the few that stay open very picturesque. In the subway stations one half the lights are out, and also in the trains themselves.
>
> It is interesting to see how gently but firmly they are taking hold of their coal problem....There is a big dealer Bernot, who has small stores scattered all over Paris, who sells one rather small bag at a time to the head of each family in each district, and it is amazing to see the queues waiting on the sidewalks to be served of surely 100 people. They have to wait and wait, and do it almost every day because they get so little at a time. Many take it home in the baby carriage.
>
> There are very snappy women conductors on the street cars and subway ticket takers. There are no motor buses but there is a wonderful resurrection of old and dilapidated horses, cabs and cabbies, all to match in decrepitude. No one is allowed to go to the theatre in evening dress. A man in a dress suit was refused admission the other night.
>
> It is also interesting to hear how these young French girls who were absolutely forbidden to put foot outside their own doors without an older person, now go to work in their hospitals at 7 in the morning and return at 7 at night solo alone. All the big hotels are partly or entirely turned into hospitals. And there are in Paris, mostly on the Champs Elysees, a Dutch, a Russian, an Italian, a Japanese, a Swedish, a Scottish hospital, etc. all for the *French* wounded.

When the United States finally declared war on Germany in the spring of 1917, she described the emotional climate surrounding her:

> I feel sort of blown up with news and excitement, but I suppose once I try to put it on paper it'll evaporate. It really is a wonderful sensation to be here these days....Griette's description of the attitude, both of the men and nurses, at her hospital was very interesting. Previous to the break, the men, disgusted by the "peace without victory," were pigheaded when she would

try and discuss things with them, the other nurses skeptical. The day of the break she suddenly acquired great glory, the men thinking she was inspired, and the girls curious to know how truly she had so much faith in America, and everyone jubilant with cheers and flags. The next day all the French people were in a state of exaltation, but the second day there seemed to be more sadness at the idea of another big country being plunged in, than unmixed joy.

When the American Red Cross arrived in France in June 1917, it planned to absorb the various relief organizations that were already working in Paris. While it offered these much money and plentiful supplies, many agencies had been in the field since 1914, whereas the Red Cross had little or no experience in the actual work going on in Paris and its environs. Moreover, many agencies were operating as branches of well-established charitable institutions in their native countries. The Red Cross met with considerable reluctance from many of the agencies, though most of them offered assistance to the newcomer. "They felt with justice," one Red Cross worker wrote, "that they had much to offer the Red Cross in the way of resources and of experience. All this they did offer, but were unwilling to give up their identity." A compromise was therefore accomplished, wherein certain agencies were designated as "departments" of the Red Cross. However, it was obvious that better cooperation and coordination was much needed among all the agencies working in civilian war relief. Margaret Curtis's foresighted plans for coordination now were recognized as valid, and the Red Cross soon gave her wide responsibilities for the overall coordination of Relief Agencies. From this time on, her affiliation with the Red Cross was official. She was appointed Assistant to the Chief of Refugee Affairs in Paris, and soon thereafter became *Chef du Bureau*. When the Battle of the Marne was raging in 1918, only 30 miles away from Paris, it was Aunt Pedge who directed operations to handle the tremendous stream of refugees pouring into the city.

Back home in Manchester, her family reacted to her promotion to Bureau chief with pride. Her sister Elinor wrote, "We are all puffed up over your importance and competence....Francie (as a School Committee Member) is nothing in comparison to you!" Her sister Hat's praise, however, was decidedly back-handed: "Goodness, Petty, are you *that* fat? All your friends on first sight of you are overcome. I'd hate to tell you what they say and write. For pity's sake, do you never take a step of exercise?...Ma gives out that you are the most important person in Paris...says 'she is a very intelligent girl.' Ho Ho Ho."

Meanwhile, Pedgy was working on another aspect of the refugee problem. Even before she became *Chef du Bureau,* she had written her family:

> I have got a bee in my bonnet now about the work. To my mind the most striking and also important need that we see among our families is better living arrangements and to get them out of the demoralizing and begging atmosphere of Paris. I can't see why we can't rent small houses outside of Paris and sublet to those innumerable families whom we tell to look for lodgement and the minute they say they are refugees they are refused. My plot would be to rent them either furnished or unfurnished, and the furniture on the installment plan I haven't sprung all this on Mrs. Shurtleff yet, but it certainly is very striking and eye opening to see how much better the repatries (those who stayed on their land during the German occupation) look than the Parisian refugees—even with their tales of meagre rations.

The following year, Peg reported to her family "up to the present five societies have undertaken buildings and we have turned over to them 24 houses with *logements* for about 750 families." Later, when she was home for the summer she had a letter from a Red Cross captain:

> That housing scheme of yours has proved a splendid success. All the houses are still packed full. The rents have been paid very regularly and I have already collected over 100,000 francs from the various French organizations....The advantage of letting all leases be signed by French organizations and in letting these run the buildings, is that all such buildings are in full swing. This would probably not have been the case, had the Red Cross done all the work itself.

150

Although she came home for summers in Manchester, Aunt Pedge kept in steady touch with her work abroad, and spent part of her vacation stumping for the Red Cross, giving speeches up and down the Atlantic Coast and as far afield as Chicago. Some of these speeches, both earnest and anecdotal, were published in Red Cross journals. Here are two examples:

SOCIAL WORK IN FRANCE

I have racked my brain for a better word than "Family Relationships" to describe the things that make up the component parts of family life, but I can't find a better one. What are they? Dr. Cabot condensed these the other day into Economic, Spiritual and Physical.

At home, in charity work I have often heard said, and sometimes thought myself "How nice it would be to be trying to aid families who got into difficulties through no fault of their own." You wouldn't then have to say, "I can't give a pair of shoes here because that would leave more money for the father to spend on drink and seems to condone his drinking," or "I can't give a layette to this unmarried mother for it would seem to be making no reproof for her bad behavior," etc. etc.

The Refugees certainly cannot be said to be in their trouble through any fault of their own; we must turn to Kaiser William for the Cause of their Misery. And yet, in working with the Refugees for the last year I had it very forcibly driven into me that after all, "causes" are not the whole story, and that *Human Nature* is very much the same, whether it is American or Irish or French or whether it is peace-time or war-time. Therefore the things that we have found true in peace-time, at home, still hold true in war-time, and we are not justified in slighting them or dodging them by the excuse of such words as "Temporary," "Emergency," "Unusual Situation," "Force of Circumstances," etc. So I come back to my family relationships and its bearing on Social Work.

The above talk was probably given in 1917. But the need for Americans to understand how desperately their funding of the American Red Cross was needed came out in its "Lake Division News," in July 1918:

"The need for trained workers is inexpressibly great—in all, there are only about 2000 workers now in France from America, 2000 to help a whole nation of people, just a drop in the bucket." Earnestly Miss Margaret Curtis, Associate Chief of the Bureau of Refugees, American Red Cross in France, made this plea for seasoned social workers.

After a summer at home, bolstering the Red Cross with her speeches, and golfing again with her sister Hatty, Pedge returned to Paris in September. The war still went on, and the tragic plight of homeless civilians still continued and would continue long after Armistice Day, that famous November 11th, when all guns went silent. Aunt Hat resumed her faithful letter-writing, giving Pedgy family news in her usual terse and cryptic style:

> Jimmy is so-so—works 3 hours. Chinn does his electrical contracts job while Grace runs the cigarettes to the exclusion of everything else—dances included. Gladys is enjoying N.Y. greatly thrilled by some New Thought people! While Frère gives G1. electric treatments and then goes and gets baked-lunches and dines wi queer Westerners....

Aunt Hat also saw to it that her nieces wrote to their aunt overseas. Here is one from my sister Happy, the oldest of us five Hopkinson sisters (Maly was the next youngest; Elly and Joany, then ages eight and five, were the two youngest).

> Dear Aunt Pedge,
> This is writing before the week is up since Maly wrote, but Aunt Hat wants me to tell you a funny conversation of Elly and Jo before I forget it. Overheard when they were in Bed, and I was outside the Nursery Door.
> Elly: "...And you know Joany, the Kaiser's the king of the Germans."
> J.: "Is he? I didn't know that! Who's the King of America?"
> E: "O no, Joany, there isn't a king of America, we have a President."
> J: "Why? Did our King of America die?"
> E: "No, we've always had a president. You see, Joany, a president is *much* better than a king. You see, why a king is bad, the oldest son is always king next, and sposing the son is bad,

why there it is? A king isnt half as good as a president. The people choose who they want to have for president."

Once Joany said to me "*I* think the Germans are very selfish. They don't let other people have things. I should think they might let even the Turkeys have some vegetables and things."

Elly and Jo have these political talks almost every night when in bed, and I have stood more than once outside the door listening. It is very amusing.

Mother got up yesterday from 3 days in bed of a bad cold...

We are getting millions of grapes from the orchard.

Chloe (dog) has come back and is dreadfully cunning, though a great deal bigger than when last we saw her. She is gray now, like Joffey.

Good bye
Harriot

Plainly, even the youngest Americans knew what was going on in Europe—though all I can clearly remember about the War was that when eating peaches, we saved the stones to be ground up and used in gas masks.

Aunt Pedge's work in Paris continued unceasingly, these last months of the war, and long afterwards. The devastation of normal civilian life in most of Northern France had been nearly complete. Refugees no longer streamed into Paris, but uprooted families returning to their home villages and farmland found little shelter in houses turned to rubble, and nothing to eat in gardens turned to wasteland. Resettling these war-shattered people and providing food for them was a monumental task, requiring much experienced knowledge, much skillful organizing of all available resources, and an unfailing capacity for hard labor. Aunt Pedge met all these requirements. Moreover, she possessed infinite patience and faced each new predicament with friendly and deliberate composure. Her outstanding work, steady and great-hearted through war and its aftermath, won recognition not only throughout the many relief agencies she worked with. Margaret Curtis, the American volunteer, was awarded the *Légion d'Honneur,* the highest citation that could be bestowed on a civilian by the Government of France.

During the spring of 1919, Aunt Pedge traveled through the countryside setting up small warehouses to serve as distribution centers, supplying goods to help returning families start life again at home. She and her fellow-workers were much impressed with these staunch French people, the bravery and good will with which they began again: "I got back yesterday afternoon," she writes,

> after what seems to me the most interesting four day motor trip I've had since I've been in France. When I said so this morning at breakfast, the boys naturally wanted to know why, and I was a little put to it to explain, but I think it was on account of the variety of experiences and the feeling that we were giving very real pleasure and were wanted....To hop airily from the first night in a French chateau, now a Colonel's headquarters, to the last night in a freight car with pig troughs, bicycles and mattresses festooned around you, and the two intervening nights spent one on a German operating table and the other with a French laundress who wouldn't take my pay because the Americans were their deliverers, gives an idea of the whole plot....
>
> ...In almost all the destroyed villages we went through we would come on groups of German prisoners clearing up ruins, putting make-shift planks in for doors and shutters, or putting on tiles, but that was our first time of coming across goodsized detachments of French soldiers, and they were picturesque enough in their blue uniforms, working in the fields up the sloping hillsides. We stopped and asked what it meant, and it appears that they have now turned in the parts of the army that have horses, to help in the agricultural work. These were heavy artillery!...

After her four years and more in France, both during the war and afterwards, Aunt Pedge spent some time at home. But in 1921, she went back to Europe. World War I had brought destruction and upheaval in many countries, and people who had lost their homes and way of life were on the move, still desperately needing assistance. Relief agencies were at work here and there throughout Europe during the long-drawn out period of reconstruction. Margaret Curtis, now an experienced worker and administrator in refugee affairs, joined up with the active service of the Society of Friends in setting up health clinics, in Austria, Poland and Czechoslovakia. She writes:

> Warsaw is quite a big showy city....The streets are crowded with people—most of them extraordinarily well shod, but there are slews of beggars, particularly around church doors. Every other person is in some part of a uniform—mostly ex-American which doesn't mean that they are in the Army the least little bit in the world. But still there are lots of soldiers around, in every kind of imaginable uniform, and the police carry a gun. The children that you see look white and peeked, but not shockingly so.
>
> We visited the Headquarters of the Russian Red Cross, and it was a nightmare. Horribly jammed in an ouvrier, a squalid restaurant for "Intelligentsia" and an awful canteen for kids— eight women were squashed into a coal hole, paring potatoes; three were teachers, and awful looking wrecks...blue hands everywhere, and to cap the climax, an old lady had gone crazy and was clutching our arms, begging rags. The Poles hate 'em — and they can't go back to Russia, even if they could live there, once they crossed the border....In the P.M. we visited the most perfectly appointed laboratory I have ever imagined. For completeness it has the Rockefeller Institute beaten a mile. It is under the government with a Jewish Dr. Wrackman at its head. He's a wizard, Dr. Emerson says....I had a long and satisfactory going over of things with Mr. Fogg, the head of the Quakers. I hope that a trip he suggested with one of the inspectors in a camion out to the eastward will materialize...I am probably leaving Friday night with Dr. Taylor (Medical Director) and Miss Matthews (Head Nurse) for Cracow. The American Red Cross has some cars that they have stripped and put beds in and can hitch on to any old train—and that's what we are going in apparently.

But southwards, in the Balkans and Asia Minor, war was not over. In 1920 it flared again, between Greece and Turkey. Turkey, fighting to regain territory lost by terms of post-war treaties, was taking over all of Anatolia: to the East, the Armenians had undergone the first big holocaust of the 20th century;

to the West, the Turks attempted to take over the Aegean seaports and land that had been home to the Greeks since classical times. When the ancient city of Smyrna was burned to the ground, the Greeks were driven into the sea.

In Athens, a number of relief agencies formed a Disaster Relief Commission to try to meet the needs of thousands of Greeks arriving in their tragic exodus from Asia Minor. And of course Aunt Pedge was there to join in the Commission's task. She worked in Greece until the spring of 1923, when, having been told of her mother's death, she came home.

Soon she was immersed again in the activities of the Boston Family Welfare Society. She had served there as a social worker when she first started her career. She was now a member of the Board of Directors. Her experiences in Europe coupled with her innate good judgment made her invaluable, and her opinions were much respected. She remained an active presence on the Board for the next thirty years, taking on a variety of responsibilities, from Finance Secretary to Chairman of the Board. Besides the Family Welfare Society, Aunt Pedge also took up her familiar task of strengthening support for the Maverick Dispensary in East Boston, which Aunt Hat had valiantly sustained during her absence, not only by appealing for donations by annual letter, but by dashing over to help out the clinic's shorthanded staff.

But the refugee problem in Europe was not over, even five years after the Versailles Treaty had been signed. People of war-torn countries were still wandering, uprooted families were struggling to keep together while the breadwinner searched for some sort of livelihood, if not in his own country, then in some less devastated area. Plainly, an international agency was needed, to facilitate opportunities for potential workers currently adrift, to help reunite families and resettle them in a new land. Margaret Curtis was soon abroad again, in Geneva, as one of the three founders of the International Migration Service. In 1925, she was called upon to set up an American Branch of the I.M.S., in New York. By 1928, the League of Nations asked I.M.S. delegates to serve on its Committee of Experts on Assistance to

Indigent Aliens. For the next twelve years U.S. delegates served on this Committee, and often presided at its meetings. Peg wrote to her sisters after a 1929 session:

> Well, Geneva went well—after dreading the presiding and the whole do—I quite enjoyed it, and we had an impressive number of *men* from the IMS committees in different countries, including the vice president of the Polish Senate and the head of the Department of Emigrants, the Ministry of the Interior from Czechoslovakia—and a Czech Consul General—and all went well and on time!

Her organizing skills were called upon again, back in Boston, when during the Great Depression years, many charitable agencies, large and small, were unable to raise sufficient funds individually to keep their operations going. In 1935, they met the crisis by joining together in one great financial drive. The money raised by this massive effort was then allotted appropriately among them. Margaret Curtis was appointed Director of the Women's Division in this Emergency Campaign.

She returned to Europe in 1939, on a mission linking I.M.S. work with an Advisory Board to President Roosevelt on a Special Children's Project for providing American homes for refugee children. Once more, she was in an atmosphere she remembered all too well. Hitler had already annexed Danzig and the Polish Corridor when her work took her to Germany:

> A personal nightmare—not just for the Europeans, and every day such a build-up for war. Constant comparison between Aug. 1914 and 1939....The night we left Berlin for Stuttgart there was a broadcast from Danzig. Every Berlin radio had to be on, and in our hotel all business stopped....If anyone spoke in a normal voice, they were shushed as though it were a prayer meeting—and people from the street came in to hear. Outside it was extraordinary—scarcely a wheel turning except pairs of secret police on bicycles and on foot, everywhere. You never heard or saw such posters against the British—and we were told of, but didn't see, little billets-doux of what happened to spies and particularly foreign women that they said would make your teeth chatter....

During the years of World War II, Aunt Pedge was active on the home front. A member of the War Production Board from 1942 to 1945, she was chairman of the Women's Division in Massachusetts, working on its Salvage Committee. Households were urged to save all used metals, particularly tin cans, and all used cooking fats, since these were needed by the War Department for weapons production. Her appeals in local papers were effective:

Open Letter to the Housewives of Massachusetts

Will you save *all* your fats? Will you save the skin off soups and the trimmings from meats and the drippings from all roasts? Will you save even the fat left on plates as well as in pans, and help us reach our quota in the months ahead?

Yours to roast, baste and pan the enemy

She was also in charge of placing European children in Massachusetts homes. Many of these were English children, sent by their parents to be safely away from the bombing of London. These were welcomed into American families, and most stayed on for the duration of the War. Aunt Pedge took particular interest in one family of a mother and four children, settling them on the Manchester estate, in Mr. Hooper's old house. Her care and kindness have never been forgotten by Elaine Campbell-Jones, the mother, who even four decades later always writes of "Aunt Pedge," in her annual Christmas greeting from Bath, England.

Always devoted to the Manchester place, Aunt Pedge began to busy herself more and more with its upkeep. During the war, when most young men were away in uniform, it was hard to find an able worker to help Mr. Scott, the caretaker, with the many and varied tasks needing to be done. Aunt Pedge borrowed the old white horse from the Poor Farm nearby and hitched it to the plough. All the next week she plodded back and forth across the wide and generous acreage of the vegetable garden, turning over the soil, preparing it for the summer's crops. As the family's handyman, she was an adept carpenter, and kept a basket of tools in the dining-room. It stood next to that magnificent MacIntire chest-on-chest already described in the last chapter as being used as a receptacle for ripening fruit. Aunt Pedge kept her larger saws, and boxes of tacks and nails in the aristocratic mahogany drawers, along with the aforementioned pears. As for leaky plumbing, stubborn windowframes and faltering electric lights, she made it her business to take care of them, only occasionally calling in a professional to take over the job.

Another useful role Aunt Pedge assumed was that of family chauffeur. Aunt Fan, getting old, wisely gave up driving; Aunt Bog had never learnt to drive, and Aunt Hat, after her near-fatal accident, never put herself behind a steering wheel again. Pedgy and her car thus became indispensable. And how she loved this role! It meant not only that she could be kindly and generous in running errands for others; it also put her, the youngest of the sisters, in a dominant position, since the others depended on her daily. The Sharksmouth estate being almost two miles away from the center of Manchester, Aunt Pedge drove to the post office every morning to collect the mail and newspaper. She made additional trips during the day, doing errands or taking people to and from the railroad station. And of course, whenever a long trip to New Hampshire and elsewhere was planned, Pedgy took complete charge.

She had always been fascinated by automobiles, ever since they began to appear on roads. First she was charmed by a little Hupmobile, which really belonged to her friend Mabel, but Pedge took care of it. Later, she had a series of Franklins, and when not driving the current one, she spent time puttering over it in the garage. Her vehicle during the latter decade of her life was usually a Ford sedan. A dome of red glass, about four inches tall was installed on its roof, making it look almost as official as a police car. Whenever she turned in a used car, she had the dome transferred to the new one. Though she said she only had the dome so that she could easily identify the car in a crowded parking lot, one somehow felt it was more important to her as a sign of authority. Truly, in Aunt Pedge was a curious mixture of motivations: infinite kindly caring and need to dominate.

A dramatic example of this mixture occurred one day when fire broke out in the woods at Manchester. When I heard the clanging fire engines coming up our way from the town, and smelled smoke, I rushed from our house over past the Stone House, to the Cottage, crowning the ridge. Fire was creeping up the slope from the sea. Fanned by an ocean breeze, it made torch after leaping torch of the pine trees, then crept along the ground, flickering and smouldering through pine-needles and blueberry-bushes in a milky blanket of smoke.

Fire hoses writhed like boa constrictors up the long avenue and over the crest of the ridge, for they had been hitched to the hydrant down on the main road, a quarter-mile away. There were firemen everywhere. While some struggled with the coiling hose, scores were in the thick of battle. Through the crackle and hiss, the blinding smoke, the swooping torches and cracking boughs, they shouted and heaved and chopped, and shot great jets of water slanting into the inferno. And around them, little boys leapt and shouted while farther out, a ring of spectators choked and dodged, scattering when the smoke and spraying water shifted, for it seemed as if half the town had heard the fire-engines and followed them. Over all the turmoil, the fire department's auxiliary pump whanged and roared with a maddening steady rhythm, as it whipped up the pulse-rate in the already turgid hoselines.

In the center of a blackened patch stood two figures. One was the Fire Chief, doing his best to direct his men. The other was Aunt Pedge. She seemed like an elderly Valkyrie, feet planted fearlessly in the smoking turf. Her blue eyes shone imperatively at the beleaguered chief, while she spoke clearly and steadily in the unruffled tone of authority.

"Look here a minute, Chief. Stop your men. We must get this organized. What are you planning to do?"

The Chief's eyes swerved politely for a moment. "Madam, we are doing the best we can, already."

"But look here. We have a system all worked out. We have a hydrant right there—right THERE, below that ledge. Tell your men to hitch up the hose to it immediately."

160

"Madam, the hose is already hitched up."

"But there's no need to use the hydrant down on the public road. We put in ours for just this sort of emergency. You see, my brother Greely, back in 1910..."

"George, soak that briar patch before it reaches the big pine over to your right—yes, Madam?"

"We have a system all worked out. You can count on it." Her voice sharpened as she watched another beloved pine tree begin to crackle, but she slowed her words more impressively. "Chief. You've got to pay attention to me. We've got to get this fire out before it spoils the whole place, and it can be done. I'm telling you, we foresaw this a long time ago. My brother..."

"Manuel, watch it over by the big rock—better keep her playing steady on the oak tree." The Chief's competent eye watched the giant nozzle swing round till a torrent of spray drowned this new outcrop of flames.

"Chief, you'll never do it this way. My brother was in the Boston Fire Department from 1894 to '99, and he always said that water pressure was the important thing. Now our hydrant is placed so that..."

"Madam, we have all the water pressure we can use." The Chief left the charred ground and plunged into the fighting himself.

But still Aunt Pedge stood there. Her need to dominate had almost destroyed what she loved and had cherished all her life: her home surroundings at Manchester. She seemed quite unaware of this; while the fire department fought on, gradually subduing the terrible flames, she continued her train of thought. "It's curious. We never did get around to putting in that hydrant until 1916. Of course, Fan wanted it put down in the Old Orchard—she didn't want these blueberry patches meddled with. But Stivits and I knew that with the wind off the water and the angle of the slope, this was the right spot. Stivits was always right. How pleased he'd be to know he was right this time, too. He was always one for tackling things with astounding ingenuity, even when it meant innovations." The silence around her finally brought her mind into focus with her eyes. The fire was out, the crowd vanished, the firemen and engines gone. They had managed to put it out, but I knew she still thought her way would have been better.

When Aunt Pedge so unwittingly fanned the flames of that terrible fire she was in her mid-sixties. But all her life she had taken actions with total disregard of her personal feelings. She moved decisively and objectively in the outside world, doubtless never recognizing that inner world of subjective motivations, other than her wish to be helpful. Whether playing golf or working tirelessly for the down-trodden, her pre-Freudian approach was outstandingly effective. During those years of championship golf, it surely enabled her to concentrate single-mindedly on that little white ball at her feet and whack it squarely. During those years of social work, she moved from subordinate to supervisor, from board-member to chairman in many charitable endeavors both local and international, for she could be completely relied on to meet every problem with this same single-minded approach, coupled with unfailing good will.

I, too, had occasion to turn to Aunt Pedge once, during World War II when my spirits were feeling particularly battered. My husband was overseas, with the Massachusetts General Hospital Unit, and I had not seen him for three years; our four children were growing at a rapid and attention-needing pace. I was emotionally rampant and physically exhausted. Then I thought of Aunt Pedge. Would she like to go off to Maine for a three-day walking trip? She said yes. We went. We walked along the shore; we explored villages; we rowed a boat. We examined antique fire-places and roof structures. We talked about dogs, schooners and early building methods, and never once spoke about personal feelings. I came home ready to take up the four children's lives again with serenity. Aunt Pedge and I never mentioned this little vacation episode to each other afterwards. No need.

Before going any further in this account of Aunt Pedge, we should return to her golfing activities, for golf was the most enduring interest of her life. After first swinging a golf club at the age of nine, she kept right on swinging for seven decades. At the age of thirteen, as already mentioned, she played in the U.S.G.A. Women's Championship matches, qualifying 4th in a field of 29 before she was beaten by the three-time champion; then came those years when she and her sister Hat entered tournaments up and down the Eastern seaboard before they both reached the pinnacle. Aunt Hat, however, was National Women's Golf Champion of America only once, while Aunt Pedge was the national champion three times. Although she kept on playing tournament golf (and frequently winning tournaments here and there) for several decades, she was an earnest promoter of women's golf in general. In 1927, Harriot and Margaret Curtis developed plans for an international tournament, which would bring together women from many countries on a regular basis. On the handsome silver Curtis Cup is engraved: "to stimulate friendly rivalry among the women golfers of many lands." Establishing the tournament turned out to be a five-year process, entangled by many complications; the sisters' worldwide concept had to be whittled down somewhat. The first Curtis Cup matches were played in 1932, and the tournament has been held biennially ever since, the matches played alternately in Great Britain and the United States. The Curtis Cup now stands high and solidly among sporting events. In fact, by the 1950s, it had become so popular that many would-be contenders had to be turned away one year, with the promise that they would be first on the list for the matches two years later. The *New Yorker* magazine wrote in an article titled "Ladies at Manchester" about the fourth tournament:

> Played biennially, alternately in England and America, Curtis Cup matches have for some reason always been devoid of that special kind of competitive ill will which is demonstrated so frequently in other international sporting events. Last week's series was no exception to the rule. A fair example of its harmony and good manners was supplied when, playing with Patty Berg against Jessie Anderson and Elsie Corlett, Glenna Collett Vare absentmindedly used her toe to test the consistency of the sand in a trap before making an explosion shot that landed within six feet of the pin. Mrs. Vare readily admitted her

mistake when the referee called her attention to it. Several minutes passed before her opponents could be persuaded to accept the obligatory penalty....

Aunt Pedge was very interested, also, in promoting golf for teenagers, and in 1930 she initiated the Massachusetts girls' Junior Championship. The trophy she donated was in the shape of a daisy, the winning girls' names to be engraved on its petals.

Many years later, she promoted another sort of golfing activity. This was a form of "golf therapy" for the men at the Veterans Hospital in Bedford. Initially, she brought to the hospital some two- to three hundred used balls and a few clubs, so that the more active veterans could practice driving. This became so popular that the hospital established a five-hole golf course on the grounds. And why did Aunt Pedge have so many used balls on hand? Because as she approached old age she began to lose interest in playing a full eighteen-hole round of golf, but still loved to spend some time on the links of the Essex County Club, the scene of so many of her triumphs. As the Club grounds are halfway between Sharksmouth and the town, she was apt to stop by on her way home from the Manchester post office and spend an hour or so strolling about, looking for lost balls. Monday mornings were particularly rewarding, after the many foursomes played during the weekend. Down along the brook was the most fruitful area, but the rough, bordering the fairways, was also good hunting ground. It was easy to spot abandoned balls in the brook and its muddy banks; the treasure in the long grass was more of a challenge. She met this by lying down and rolling until she felt a bump under her. Although she knew this was a somewhat idiosyncratic act, she often described it, even at golfers' meetings. As three times National Champion and four times winner of the Massachusetts women's golf crown, she was often asked to speak at these gatherings; she would reminisce happily, for she loved an audience. And audiences loved her, for she was now the Grand Old Lady of Golf. She had quite a few anecdotes to relate which she called her "silly-billies." These she told with impressive deliberation—until she reached the dramatic finale, with an appreciative laughing bark of her own, which gave her listeners their clue for laughter. One tale often repeated was about that first tournament, when she was a plump thirteen-year-old. When her vanquished opponent was asked, "How *could* you have allowed that child to beat you?", she replied, "She's not a child—she's a Baby Grand!" Another favorite, repeated many times after she had reached her very late seventies, went this way: "I was playing in a match at the Rockport Golf Club, a couple of years ago. I was pretty old at the time, and was certainly off my game, that day. As I walked from the fourth tee, I remarked to my caddy, 'You might find it hard to believe, but once I was pretty good. I won the United States Championship.' 'Oh,' he said, "Who'd you beat? The Russians?'" Then came her short, sharp bark, followed by the chorus of laughter. (I always joined in, if I were present, but I was never sure wherein the humor of the punch-line lay.)

Aunt Pedge was a good subject for occasional newspaper articles all her life. This pleased her, for as the youngest in that great family of ten children, her need for recognition must have started quite early. Besides pictures of her, and write-ups on the sports pages, her work during World War I drew attention. "Golfing champion now Red Cross worker in France," the *Boston Herald* announces with a picture, and later on, "Boston Woman cares for 78 Refugee Casualties single-handed during Blitz of Paris" is the headline for a story. A couple of decades later, the *Herald* published a big picture of her, the caption below it asking "Who won U.S. titles in both Golf and Tennis the same year? MARGARET CURTIS, only American male or female to perform Feat." But during the 1950s, when she was still playing golf though well into her seventies, she appeared again and again on sports pages. Usually she was pictured swinging a club, her smiling face above her well-bosomed sweater and saggy skirt, her shapely shins bare and muscular above her short socks and men's sport shoes. One time the caption below a picture reads, "Miss Margaret Curtis, Gracious but Dynamic;" another time the caption is merely "Continues to Lead the Way." "Champions Past and Present" shows her, an early winner of the Bobby Jones Award, standing with Joe Carr, the current recipient. In 1956, the Sunday *Herald* ran a headline four columns wide proclaiming "Science, not Fashion helps Women's Golf—MARGARET CURTIS," going on to explain her belief that proper muscular development is more important than Bermuda shorts.

In 1952 she was honored at a Sports Writers dinner. Here is a little speech she wrote out in pencil ahead of time, knowing she would have to speak:

> When I heard that Francis Ouimet and Bill Cunningham were to be here tonight I rejoiced greatly. I knew it meant fun for all of us *and* let me out of making a speech.
>
> What I *am* is easy to see. Exhibit A in the Museum of Ancient Golfers. Nevertheless, I am hoping I am not the only B.C. golfer here. B.C. before the century of course.
>
> I want to bring back some nostalgic memories if possible. I have here a few clubs. An Auchtilone Brassey—a Torgan Cleek and a niblick—whose face is nearer the size of a silver dollar than the bread-and-butter plates of the present day.
>
> And balls—dear old gutties. They are in a box that is marked Agrippa, Coventry, England. Moulded January 1900. Painted June 1900. These are balls that I or some member of my family played with.
>
> Misselborough. Ocabo. Silvertown. Vardon Flyer.
>
> And then came the Haskell rubber core, patented April 11th, 1899; in use in 1900.
>
> I'm going to end with a few foolish anecdotes.
>
> Playing in my 2nd National Championship, I played against Miss Grace Keyes of Concord. I was 16, and very green. She laid me the simplest form of stymie—I was non-plussed and evidently showed it. Oh said she it's not so hard, just take your mashie and putt with it. I obeyed, and drew forth from her, "Well, am I a darn fool to tell you how to beat me?"
>
> I've had the good luck to get 2 holes-in-one. The effect on the audience is what I want to describe. The first was in Murray Bay, Canada. We caught up with 2 old codgers—one was over 80 and the other only a little younger. After they had holed out on a hole, they stood by the green and waited for us to play. I shot. And for a moment I thought they had gone crazy. I could see the flag but not the green. One threw his hat sailing up into the air

and the other let out an Indian yell. They came hurrying towards us. The Indian said "We had decided to let you through but we said who is the skirts that thinks she has to wait on a 200 yard hole? and then you put it in the hole!" By the time we finished playing the whole town had heard the tale.

The attention and admiration Margaret Curtis received in later life was particularly gratifying and helpful after the loss of her dear companion of many years. Lovely, gentle Mabel Sturgis, considerably older than herself, died when Aunt Pedge was still a vigorous seventy-year-old. No wonder she needed attention. No wonder she needed an audience for her long-winded tales and golfing anecdotes and no wonder she continued her usual round of activities, seemingly unaware of her own sense of grievous loneliness. Her life-long habits continued undisturbed. She still tackled every project, be it sport or welfare work, with thorough and optimistic concentration while leaving unrecognized emotions and personal reactions common to all humans. Of course, this was true of all the Aunts, as I have already mentioned. With them it was *de rigueur* to carry out daily activities and sisterly chit-chat at home with no outward expression of inner feelings. Though Aunt Bog had her outbursts, these were considered abnormal by her sisters. Aunt Pedge, however, seemed to have gone further than the rest in non-recognition of self. This gap in her comprehension appeared very clearly one day in Manchester, when I went over the Aunts' house. The room opening from the living-room had once been the Library, but now it was solely Aunt Pedge's domain; as she had gradually taken over the management of household and family affairs from her aging sister Fan, she had gradually taken over this room as her own headquarters. Here were gathered all the objects she either was fond of or that reminded her of some episode in her past, or were broken implements and devices she planned to mend sometime. There was a magnificent view of the ocean outside the bay windows—but she habitually sat at a large mahogany table-desk to the right, where she couldn't see it. Though I had come over that August morning to ask her about some minor practical matter, I couldn't get very near her, nor could I sit down, because the floor space was almost entirely occupied by objects: golf clubs, cardboard crates and boxes piled on each other and topped with a handsaw; two broken radios (of the wooden gothic-arch vintage), a side-board picked up at some country auction but not good enough for the dining room, two other desks, and three pairs of beautiful and curious andirons (not in the fireplace, because that was already filled with other things). Books were stacked in rows, occupying a large portion of floor space, and photographs had been sorted into piles. Here was a broken lamp, there an axe. On top of a high bookcase stood a row of World War I bomb shells, flanked by early American teapots, charmingly decorated. Have I left anything out? Many things, so diverse that they cannot be catalogued: a little pile of square-sided nails; a basketful of golf balls; two pipes with tobacco pouch; a sundial, a pair of rubbers and three paint-boxes. There were three cotton hats, a tennis visor and four clocks, several with missing hands. An open box of Ritz crackers stood on the floor beside her desk, and she was munching when I arrived.

"Hi, Aunt Pedge!" said I, starting to navigate meticulously toward the mantelpiece. I had a cigarette in my hand, and planned to snuff it out at the back of the fireplace, safely beyond the boxes at its front and on the hearth. "Well, Ibb," said Aunt Pedge, laying down her pen, and watching as I stooped to reach in to the back of the fireplace. "Leave your hand right there. See that white box, just below it?" Yes, there was a smallish white cube, among the cartons. "Those are Fan's ashes. We don't know what to do with them." "Oh," I said, and then was silent.

Aunt Fan had died the August before, a full year ago. My first reaction was one of shock. I was angry, horrified and contemptuous of the Aunts' breezy, matter-of-fact handling of situations. "There must be something to do," I mumbled tentatively, and left.

Then I realized that of course they (the three remaining Aunts) could not think what to do—and had avoided thinking about it for a year. Aunt Fan, the eldest of them all, had been the mainstay, the standard bearer, the natural leader and pacesetter of the family throughout the many decades of their lives. No words of love, affection, trust and interdependence were ever spoken between the sisters. Their conversation at home was a vivid fabric of humor, opinions on current events, criticisms and witticisms, and choruses affection for their omnipresent dogs, for it was all right to lavish love overtly on canines, but never on humans. So with Aunt Fan gone, what could they do? How could they react?

As I walked away from their house, I knew it was up to us nieces to resolve the dilemma, and free the Aunts from a catastrophe that had remained stationary for a year, frozen in place not by apathy but by unacknowledged feeling. We all met the following Saturday, aunts, nieces, great-nieces-and-nephews, on the piazza of the Aunts' house. Everyone had a tale to tell about Aunt Fan, with affection, amusement, admiration. After a few anecdotes, more memories were revitalized, and we must have told a score or more to each other, sitting there in the sun, three generations together, laughing and appreciating. Then we took the little white cardboard box and buried it under the laurel trees which Aunt Fan had dug up in the neighboring town of Magnolia fifty years before. They were little saplings then; now a sturdy grove, they are covered with pink blossoms in the spring, and everybody enjoys them.

Throughout the ceremony for Aunt Fan, Aunt Pedge had remained fairly silent. Expecting she might easily meander from a sisterly reminiscence into a rambling golf saga, I had come ready to close it off gracefully by reading aloud part of an essay on "Blackberrying" by Ralph Waldo Emerson. Both subject and author were favorites of Aunt Fan's; but this was not needed, for Aunt Pedge hardly spoke a word.

In her latter years, Aunt Pedge grew more and more silent. She took to playing solitaire and sat for hours at a time puzzling over a layout of cards in front of her. She even took a pack with her when she went to visit Aunt Bog in the nursing home. Here she made no attempt at conversation with her sister and merely sat shifting her solitaire cards around on a low table near Aunt Bog's bed. It seems obvious that her faithful and frequent visits were due to compassion, and quite likely remorse for having put Aunt Bog into that nursing home in the first place. But I doubt if these motivations ever rose to the surface of her mind. Any more than they had a few years before, when I wanted to repay her for a very generous loan. When I offered her my check, she didn't put out her hand but said, "Are you sure you want to do this?" and seemed very disappointed when I forced it on her. Afterwards, I realized how lonely she was, and how she had needed this bond both as a token of love and as a way of keeping a controlling hand in my affairs and a place in my life.

She played more and more solitaire as time went on, but gradually, rather than enjoying her game, she seemed more anxious about it. Her brows would furrow, and she often scowled. Glancing at her from across the room, while chatting with Aunt Hat, one realized she was deeply puzzled. But she never spoke.

When Aunt Pedge didn't come down to breakfast on Christmas morning in 1965, Aunt Hat went up to see why not. She found her lifeless in her bed. Whereas the other aunts all lived to be well into their nineties, Aunt Pedge was only eighty-two, that Christmas morning.

But what a lot she had done! What a lot she had contributed to her fellow humans—not with charm, not with gaiety, but with hard work, deep concern, and untiring good will. And what was her hunger for approval but a need for love? A need unrecognized by her, of course.

❧

Envoi

Boston has long been renowned for its special breed of women. Many people have smiled over that one who was asked where she usually bought her hats, and replied, "We have our hats." Even Californians are familiar with the breed, because of that woman who was asked, on arrival, what route she had taken driving across the country, and had replied, "We came by way of Dedham," (a town twelve miles west of Boston). Less well-known is the dear elderly dowager who spent her winters in Boston, and every morning held an egg from her country estate in a teaspoon under the hot-water faucet in her Hotel Vendome suite until it was suitably soft-boiled for her breakfast. Then there was Amy Lowell, the cigar-smoking poetess, and in contrast to her, the lovely black-eyed octogenarian spinster named corespondent in the divorce proceedings of a pair of forty-year-olds. All these women of diverse traits have one characteristic in common: an ability to think, live and act as individuals, sometimes in harmony with community opinions, sometimes not. Indeed, there is a certain assured quirkiness in Bostonian females. They don't swing with every tide.

Certainly the Curtis sisters of Beacon Hill were of this special breed of individualists, as they plucked treasure from neighbors' trash-cans, used a cast-off maid's uniform for winter under- wear, and intertwined a rope of F.W. Woolworth pearls with a family heirloom when going to a dinner party. But the Aunts were not merely eccentric Bostonians. They were comfortably secure in both wealth and lineage, but they were not simply "lady bountifuls," practicing noblesse oblige. They were hard workers in the world of civic affairs, education and philan- thropic causes.

It was a man's world that the Aunts worked in. Women's suffrage was still thirty years away when they began, and the

171

present surge for women's liberation and equality was still unborn by a good sixty years. The Aunts didn't care at all; they never felt they had to fulfil some idea of women's destiny. Far from being repudiated, they were welcomed into the man's world. Government officials and fellow-workers alike applauded their deeds, sought out their advice, and enjoyed their companionship both at work and when skating together on the Charles River.

So, Aunts Fan, Bog, Hat and Pedge, I salute you, with gratitude for the abundant care and affection you gave me; with admiration for your ever-faithful work for the betterment of mankind; with pride for your accomplishments in a man's world. You didn't have to earn your living. You simply did what obviously needed doing and did it wholeheartedly.

The Five Sisters, 1938

Acknowledgements

A number of people have helped me since I started writing this book. Gertrude Prosser gave me wise and professional criticism, as did Elizabeth Becker. Elinor Appel Rockhold put in many hours of research; Beth Halsted Paddock, my granddaughter, spent hours designing the Family Tree; and Ethel Blake was truly supportive. My four children, Nell, Tom, Charles and Bella, spurred me on, and Tom and Bella were particularly helpful, as they not only gave me frank editorial criticism, but saw this book through to publication.

Isabella Halsted

The Author

The typeface is Sabon.
Most of the photographs were taken by
Mrs. Greely S. Curtis and Isabella Curtis; they were selected and
arranged by Bella Halsted; some dates are perforce approximations.

The text of this book is printed on recycled paper

The "Family Tree," c. 1885

Curtis Family Tree

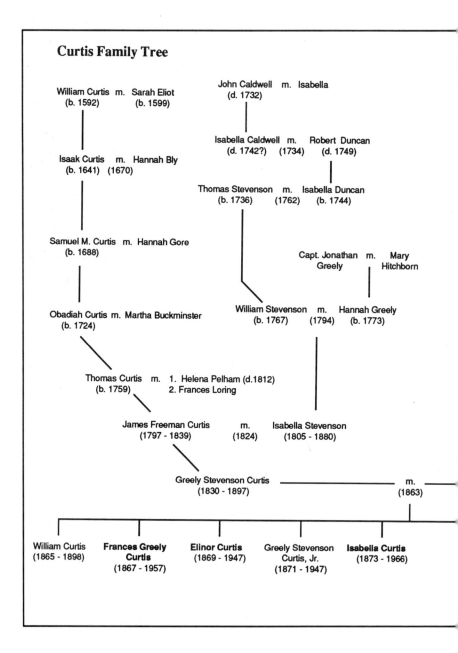

William Curtis m. Sarah Eliot
(b. 1592)   (b. 1599)

John Caldwell   m. Isabella
(d. 1732)

Isaak Curtis   m. Hannah Bly
(b. 1641)   (1670)

Isabella Caldwell m.   Robert Duncan
(d. 1742?)   (1734)   (d. 1749)

Thomas Stevenson   m.   Isabella Duncan
(b. 1736)   (1762)   (b. 1744)

Samuel M. Curtis   m. Hannah Gore
(b. 1688)

Capt. Jonathan   m.   Mary
Greely   Hitchborn

Obadiah Curtis m. Martha Buckminster
(b. 1724)

William Stevenson   m.   Hannah Greely
(b. 1767)   (1794)   (b. 1773)

Thomas Curtis   m.   1. Helena Pelham (d.1812)
(b. 1759)   2. Frances Loring

James Freeman Curtis   m.   Isabella Stevenson
(1797 - 1839)   (1824)   (1805 - 1880)

Greely Stevenson Curtis ——————————————— m. ——
(1830 - 1897)   (1863)

William Curtis   Frances Greely   Elinor Curtis   Greely Stevenson   Isabella Curtis
(1865 - 1898)   Curtis   (1869 - 1947)   Curtis, Jr.   (1873 - 1966)
                       (1867 - 1957)   (1871 - 1947)

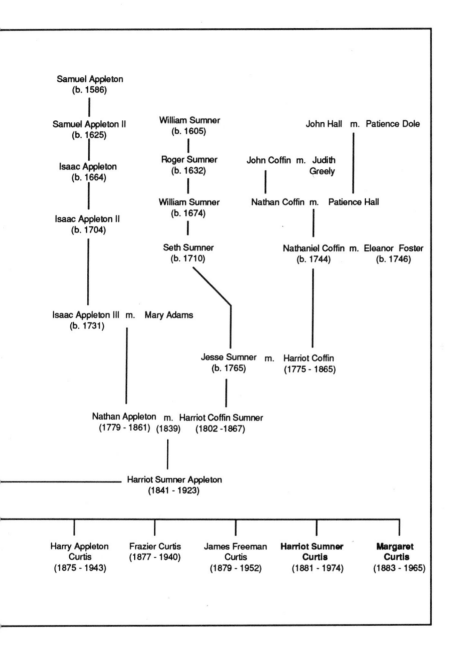

Samuel Appleton
(b. 1586)

Samuel Appleton II
(b. 1625)

William Sumner
(b. 1605)

John Hall   m. Patience Dole

Isaac Appleton
(b. 1664)

Roger Sumner
(b. 1632)

John Coffin m.   Judith
Greely

Isaac Appleton II
(b. 1704)

William Sumner
(b. 1674)

Nathan Coffin m.   Patience Hall

Seth Sumner
(b. 1710)

Nathaniel Coffin m. Eleanor Foster
(b. 1744)   (b. 1746)

Isaac Appleton III m.   Mary Adams
(b. 1731)

Jesse Sumner   m.   Harriot Coffin
(b. 1765)   (1775 - 1865)

Nathan Appleton   m. Harriot Coffin Sumner
(1779 - 1861) (1839)   (1802 -1867)

Harriot Sumner Appleton
(1841 - 1923)

Harry Appleton
Curtis
(1875 - 1943)

Frazier Curtis
(1877 - 1940)

James Freeman
Curtis
(1879 - 1952)

**Harriot Sumner
Curtis**
(1881 - 1974)

**Margaret
Curtis**
(1883 - 1965)